LEADERS

as

COMMUNICATORS

AND

DIPLOMATS

The Soul of Educational Leadership

Alan M. Blankstein, Paul D. Houston, Robert W. Cole, Editors

Volume 1: Engaging EVERY Learner

Volume 2: Out-of-the-Box Leadership

Volume 3: Sustaining Professional Learning Communities

Volume 4: Spirituality in Educational Leadership

Volume 5: Building Sustainable Leadership Capacity

Volume 6: Leaders as Communicators and Diplomats

Volume 7: Data-Enhanced Leadership

Volume 8: Leadership for Family and Community Involvement

Volume 9: Leadership for Social Justice and Democracy in Our Schools

Volume 10: Redefining the Role of the Leader: Best Practices Worldwide

Volume 11: Leadership for 21st Century Schools

Volume 12: Transparent Leadership

Volume 13: Looking to the Future

THE SOUL OF EDUCATIONAL LEADERSHIP

VOLUME 6

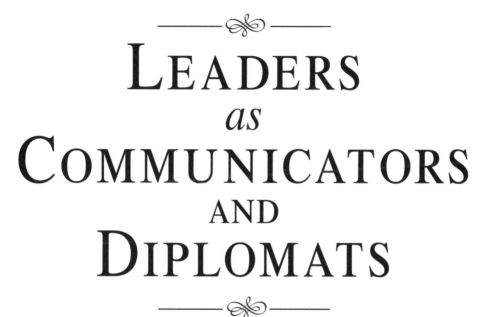

LEADERS
as
COMMUNICATORS
AND
DIPLOMATS

PAUL D. HOUSTON ❧ ALAN M. BLANKSTEIN ❧ ROBERT W. COLE

EDITORS

A JOINT PUBLICATION

CORWIN PRESS

HOPE Foundation

American Association of
School Administrators

CORWIN PRESS
A SAGE Company
Thousand Oaks, CA 91320

For information:

Corwin
A SAGE Company
2455 Teller Road
Thousand Oaks, California 91320
(800) 233-9936
Fax: (800) 417-2466
www.corwinpress.com

SAGE India Pvt. Ltd.
B 1/I 1 Mohan Cooperative
Industrial Area
Mathura Road,
    New Delhi 110 044
India

SAGE Ltd.
1 Oliver's Yard
55 City Road
London EC1Y 1SP
United Kingdom

SAGE Asia-Pacific Pte. Ltd.
33 Pekin Street #02-01
Far East Square
Singapore 048763

Printed in the United States of America.

Library of Congress Cataloging-in-Publication Data

Leaders as communicators and diplomats/editors, Paul D. Houston, Alan M. Blankstein, Robert W. Cole.
        p. cm.—(Soul of educational leadership series; v. 6)
"A joint publication with the HOPE Foundation and The American Association of School Administrators."
Includes bibliographical references and index.
ISBN 978-1-4129-4943-9 (cloth)
ISBN 978-1-4129-4944-6 (pbk.)
    1. Educational leadership—United States. 2. Communication in education—United States. 3. School superintendents—United States. I. Houston, Paul D. II. Blankstein, Alan M., 1959- III. Cole, Robert W. IV. Title. V. Series.

LB2807.L43 2009
371.2—dc22   2008049660

This book is printed on acid-free paper.

09   10   11   12   13   10   9   8   7   6   5   4   3   2   1

Acquisitions Editor:	Arnis Burvikovs
Associate Editor:	Desirée A. Bartlett
Production Editor:	Libby Larson
Copy Editor:	Teresa Herlinger
Typesetter:	C&M Digitals (P) Ltd.
Proofreader:	Theresa Kay
Indexer:	Maria Sosnowski
Cover Designer:	Michael Dubowe

CONTENTS

PREFACE

ROBERT W. COLE

L eaders don't lead alone. Leadership necessarily involves followers—people who buy into the leader's vision of where the whole bandwagon is headed. Leadership doesn't just happen, and it's hard to teach. The best leaders relate to their followers and work at understanding them. They know how to bring people together in common cause. They invoke a higher moral authority. They are storytellers, persuaders, conveners, reframers.

Our most powerful leaders speak to the hearts, the minds, and the souls of those they would lead. In the enormously demanding work of education (as Paul Houston—one of the editors of this series, together with myself and Alan Blankstein—pointed out in Volume 4, *Spirituality in Educational Leadership*), "the work we do is really more of a calling and a mission than it is a job." Our calling, whether we lead or follow, is to prepare young people for life.

The volume that opened *The Soul of Educational Leadership* series, *Engaging Every Learner*, was selected to send a signal of all-inclusiveness. Every student matters deeply, to all of us in and around schools and in our society. Volume 2, *Out-of-the-Box Leadership*, called for transformative leadership, which can come only by thinking differently about the problems and challenges we face. Volume 3, *Sustaining Learning Communities*, looked beyond inclusiveness and transformation to how best to work together to create learning communities that support enduring change. And in Volume 4, Paul Houston observed, "These jobs of ours as educational leaders are difficult and draining. They sap our physical and moral energy. We have to find ways of replenishing the supply."

Replenishing our supply is what this series is all about. From the beginning, we have aimed to provide contributions from leading thinkers and practitioners on the soul-work of educational leadership. In this volume, *Leaders as Communicators and Diplomats*, we have enlisted, among others, five superintendents or former superintendents—one of whom was named National Superintendent of the Year and one who was State Superintendent of the Year—as well as the former head of the American Association of School Administrators (AASA) and the head of the National School Public Relations Association (NSPRA).

In "The Superintendent as Communicator and Diplomat," Paul D. Houston (recently retired AASA executive director) sets the tone for the volume by observing that leaders in education must lead even in the absence of authority and power. The leader's biggest tool, according to Houston, is "the ability to communicate clearly and persuasively to the staff, and to the public and policy makers, about what the issues are and how they must be handled." Leaders must listen both with their ears and with their heart. Along the way, diplomacy comes into play: True leaders respect people, show their respect, and work with their followers for a better outcome.

"As a rookie superintendent I quickly learned that all that goes right and all that goes wrong in a school district ultimately can be traced back to communication—or a lack thereof," writes Krista Parent, superintendent of the South Lane School District in Oregon (and the 2007 National Superintendent of the Year). In "The Leader as Communicator and Diplomat," she lays out a refreshingly specific strategic plan for creating a dynamic, effective districtwide communication system, with the superintendent at its hub. Her caution is this: "If your communication system is a 'reactive' one, it is time to rethink your plan."

John R. Hoyle, professor of educational administration at Texas A&M University, tunes into the concerns at the heart of this series when he writes, "America definitely needs school leaders with heart and soul, but leaders also need skills in communicating and influencing policy makers about necessary changes in school policy to promote equity and justice for all children." In Chapter 3, "The Educational Leader: Diplomat and Communicator for All Students," Hoyle (selected in a 2004 national survey as one of four "exceptional living scholars" in educational leadership) counsels programs of leadership education "first to recruit individuals who lead with soul and have a record of success in various leadership capacities, and then to teach these individuals the skills to manage effective schools and school districts."

In "Learning to Be a Leader," the fourth chapter in this volume, Betty Rosa provides a deeply personal, from-the-trenches account of her learnings as a principal and a superintendent in New York City. "I realized that leadership is a personal journey that allows us to connect our inner world with the world that we want to affect," Rosa writes of her career, which recently culminated in her election to a 5-year term as the Regent for the Twelfth Judicial District (Bronx County, New York). "The most important lesson for me was the importance of everyone understanding our interdependence," she reflects.

"Being successful as a superintendent will not happen if you don't make a commitment to communication," writes Rich Bagin, executive director of the National School Public Relations Association since 1992. In his chapter, "Leaders as Communicators and Ambassadors," he reports that "the most successful school com-munication programs start at the top with leaders who are committed to the importance of communication and who then make sure that all central office leaders, principals, and other supervisors follow through on that commitment. Successful superintendents are the gatekeepers when it comes to communication."

Donald A. Phillips, superintendent of Poway Unified School District (a suburban K–12 district with more than 33,000 students) and 2008 California State Superintendent of the Year, recalls a har-rowing example from his district in "The Superintendent as Key Communicator and Diplomat: A Case Study." He concludes with practical lessons for leaders, including this: "During challenging times, it is essential to stand up and be counted for what we value as system leaders and what we believe is the right thing to do—even if it is not the most popular position. Leadership, in its most difficult hour, is taking a divergent path."

Now an assistant professor of educational leadership at the University of Wyoming, Mark J. Stock created a highly popular weblog called "The Wawascene" when he was superintendent of Wawasee Community Schools in northern Indiana. In "The Superintendent as Blogger," he describes how to start blogging and writes, "Blogging is just one more tool for the communication-oriented school leader. The more avenues you can provide to educate and inform the public about the important issues that affect our schools and our children, the better chance we have of sustaining and improving our public schools."

Far more important to children's life chances in the Conceptual Age than the ability to take tests, Daniel H. Pink tells us, are "high-concept and high-touch" qualities that are tougher to quantify: imagination, joyfulness, and social dexterity. Pink, author of the *New York Times* and *BusinessWeek* bestseller *A Whole New Mind*, contributes an adaptation titled "A Whole New Mind for Schools." One lesson he poses for educators is this: "When facts become so widely available, each one becomes less valuable. What begins to matter more is the ability to place these facts in *context* and to deliver them with *emotional impact*."

Finally, in an Endnote to this volume, Edward B. Fiske, former education editor of the *New York Times*, writes, "I like the notion with which this volume opened: namely that, unlike their counterparts in the business world, school leaders lack the power to control their raw materials. I tend to think of their power as comparable to that of governors and college presidents—the power not to control but to set agendas and to persuade." Author of the best-selling annual *Fiske Guide to Colleges*, he concludes that leaders in education "need powerful communication skills to carry out their jobs, and they will be most successful when they use the power of their words and images in the service of a vision of where our country's education system has been, where it is now, and where it is going."

Two years ago, at the beginning of this series, Alan Blankstein sounded the theme that continues to guide our effort: "Saving young people from failure in school is equivalent to saving their lives!" We know how to do what needs doing; research and innumerable examples of best practice have illuminated the way. As always, it is our aim to help strengthen you for this vitally important task.

ACKNOWLEDGMENTS

Corwin gratefully acknowledges the contributions of the following individuals:

Chuck Bonner, Assistant Principal
Great Valley High School
Malvern, PA

Kermit Buckner, Professor
Department of Educational Leadership
East Carolina University
Greenville, NC

Shelby Cosner, Assistant Professor
University of Illinois at Chicago
Chicago, IL

Ralph A. Gilchrest III, Principal
Lake Gibson High School
Lakeland, FL

Paul G. Young, Executive Director
West After School Center
Lancaster, OH

ABOUT THE EDITORS

Paul D. Houston served as executive director of the American Association of School Administrators (AASA) from 1994 to 2008. He currently serves as president of the Center for Empowered Leadership (CFEL).

Dr. Houston has established himself as one of the leading spokespersons for American education through his extensive speaking engagements, published articles, and his regular appearances on national radio and television.

Dr. Houston has coauthored three books: *Exploding the Myths,* with Joe Schneider; *The Board-Savvy Superintendent,* with Doug Eadie; and *The Spiritual Dimension of Leadership,* with Steven Sokolow. He has also authored three books: *Articles of Faith and Hope for Public Education, Outlooks and Perspectives on American Education,* and *No Challenge Left Behind: Transforming America's Schools Through Heart and Soul.*

He served previously as a teacher and building administrator in North Carolina and New Jersey. He has also served as assistant superintendent in Birmingham, Alabama, and as superintendent of schools in Princeton, New Jersey; Tucson, Arizona; and Riverside, California.

Dr. Houston has also served in an adjunct capacity for the University of North Carolina, Harvard University, Brigham Young University, and Princeton University. He has been a consultant and speaker throughout the United States and overseas, and he has published more than 200 articles in professional journals.

Alan M. Blankstein is founder and president of the HOPE Foundation, a not-for-profit organization whose honorary chair is Nobel Prize winner Archbishop Desmond Tutu. The HOPE Foundation (Harnessing Optimism and Potential through Education) is dedicated to supporting educational leaders over time in creating school cultures where failure is not an option for any student. HOPE sustains student success.

The HOPE Foundation brought W. Edwards Deming and his work to light in educational circles, beginning with the Shaping Chicago's Future conference in 1988. From 1988 to 1992, in a series of Shaping America's Future forums and PBS video conferences, he brought together scores of national and world leaders including Al Shanker; Peter Senge; Mary Futrell; Linda Darling-Hammond; Ed Zigler; and CEOs of GM, Ford, and other corporations to determine how best to bring quality concepts and those of "learning organizations" to bear in educational systems.

The HOPE Foundation provides professional development for thousands of educational leaders annually throughout North America and other parts of the world, including South Africa. HOPE also provides long-term support for school improvement through leadership academies and intensive on-site school change efforts, resulting in dramatic increases in student achievement in diverse settings.

A former "high risk" youth, Blankstein began his career in education as a music teacher and has worked within youth-serving organizations for 20 years, including the March of Dimes, Phi Delta Kappa, and the National Educational Service (NES), which he founded in 1987 and directed for 12 years.

He coauthored with Rick DuFour the *Reaching Today's Youth* curriculum, now provided as a course in 16 states, and has contributed writing to *Educational Leadership, The School Administrator, Executive Educator, High School Magazine, Reaching Today's Youth,* and *EQ + IQ = Best Leadership Practices for Caring and Successful Schools.* Blankstein has provided keynote presentations and workshops for virtually every major educational organization. He is author of the best-selling book *Failure Is Not an Option™: Six Principles That Guide Student Achievement in High-Performing Schools,* which has been awarded "Book of the Year" by the National Staff Development Council, and has been nominated for three other national and international awards.

Blankstein is on the Harvard International Principals Center's advisory board, has served as a board member for the Federation of Families for Children's Mental Health, is a cochair of Indiana University's Neal Marshall Black Culture Center's Community Network, and is advisor to the Faculty and Staff for Student Excellence mentoring program. He is also an advisory board member for the Forum on Race, Equity, and Human Understanding with the Monroe County Schools in Indiana, and has served on the Board of Trustees for the Jewish Child Care Agency (JCCA), at which he was once a youth-in-residence.

Robert W. Cole is proprietor and founder of Edu-Data, a firm specializing in writing, research, and publication services. He was a member of the staff of *Phi Delta Kappan* magazine for 14 years: assistant editor from 1974–1976, managing editor from 1976–1980, and editor-in-chief from 1981–1988. During his tenure as editor-in-chief, the *Kappan* earned more than 40 Distinguished Achievement Awards from the Association of Educational Publishers, three of them for his editorials.

Since leaving the *Kappan*, Cole has served as founding vice president of the Schlechty Center for Leadership in School Reform (1990–1994). In this role, he managed district- and communitywide school reform efforts and led the team that created the Kentucky Superintendents' Leadership Institute. He formed the Bluegrass Leadership Network, in which superintendents worked together to use current leadership concepts to solve reform-oriented management and leadership problems.

As senior consultant to the National Reading Styles Institute (1994–2005), Cole served as editor and lead writer of the Power Reading Program. He and a team of writers and illustrators created a series of hundreds of graded short stories, short novels, and comic books from Primer through Grade 10. Those stories were then recorded by Cole and Dr. Marie Carbo; they are now being used by schools all across the United States to teach struggling readers.

Cole has served as a book development editor for the Association for Supervision and Curriculum Development (ASCD) and for Corwin Press. He has been president of the Educational Press Association of America and a member of the EdPress Board of Directors. He has presented workshops, master classes, and lectures at universities nationwide, including Harvard University, Stanford University, Indiana University, Xavier University, Boise State University, and the University of Southern Maine. He has served as a special consultant to college and university deans in working with faculties on writing for professional publication. Recently, he began serving as managing editor and senior associate with the Center for Empowered Leadership.

ABOUT THE CONTRIBUTORS

Rich Bagin, APR, executive director of the National School Public Relations Association (NSPRA) since April 1992, has more than 30 years of experience in school and corporate public relations and communications.

In school public relations, Bagin served for 8 years as the communications director and assistant superintendent for a suburban Philadelphia school system. In that capacity, he was responsible for internal and external public relations programs and dealt with crisis situations ranging from employee strikes to federal indictments of school district architects and legal counsel. Prior to that, Bagin was a secondary school English teacher, coach, and yearbook advisor in Pennsylvania. He has also served as Director of Communications and Development for the Council of Chief State School Officers.

Bagin has conducted numerous communication audits for school districts and corporate clients. He was instrumental in initiating the NSPRA communication audit process in the mid-1980s and has authored articles on the auditing process that have appeared in various educational and communication periodicals. Bagin is the author of NSPRA's *Communication Guidebook for Teachers, Evaluating Your School Public Relations Investment, Planning Your School Public Relations Investment,* and *101 PR Ideas You Can Use Now! . . . And More!* He also authored *Principals in the Public . . . Engaging Community Support,* jointly published by MetLife, NAESP (National Elementary School Principals Association), and NSPRA. In addition, Bagin serves as a workshop leader for major education associations and school districts throughout the United States and Canada.

In the corporate sector, Bagin was senior vice president/general manager for two national and international public relations firms. He has counseled Fortune 500 firms on strategy and implemented bottom line–oriented public relations and marketing communications programs in the private sector.

Edward B. Fiske is a journalist, formerly the education editor of the *New York Times,* who is well-known for his writing on topics ranging from early childhood education in the United States to school reform in developing countries. He is author of the annual *Fiske Guide to Colleges* (Sourcebooks), which is the best-selling college guide of its kind, and numerous other books about college admissions.

After leaving the *New York Times* in 1992, Fiske lived in Cambodia, where he carried out a study of education of women and girls for the Asian Development Bank entitled "Using Both Hands." He has written extensively for UNESCO, the World Bank, USAID, the Academy for Educational Development, and other organizations with an interest in education. In addition to the *Times,* his articles have appeared in *The International Herald-Tribune, Education Week, Chronicle of Higher Education, Atlantic,* and other publications.

Fiske is married to Helen F. Ladd, a professor of public policy and economics at Duke University. Together, Fiske and Ladd have authored two books on education policy. *When Schools Compete: A Cautionary Tale* (2000) is a study of market-based school reforms in New Zealand. *Elusive Equity: Education Reform in Post-Apartheid South Africa* (2004) examines racial equity in post-apartheid South Africa. They recently edited the *Handbook on Research in Education Finance and Policy* (2007).

John R. Hoyle is professor of educational administration at Texas A&M University and specializes in leadership training and assessment and future studies. He is one of America's leading researchers and reformers in administrator training and is an authority on future studies. In a 2004 national survey, Hoyle was selected by his peers as one of four "exceptional living scholars" in educational leadership. Other honors include two Texas A&M University awards for Distinguished Achievement in Teaching; a new 2007 "Hoyle Leadership Award" created by the Texas A&M University Administrative Leadership Institute to be given to a Texas school leader who has made a positive difference in the lives of students for the betterment of society; the first "Living Legend Award" in 1999 by the National Council of Professors of Educational Administration; the 2008 Living Legend Award presented by the Texas Professors of Educational Administration; and the coveted "Golden Deeds Award" for distinguished service to Texas education. His latest book, *Leadership and Futuring: Making Visions Happen* (2007, 2nd ed.), was selected as the August 2007 Book of the Month by the National Association for Career and Technical Education. Other recent books include *The Superintendent as CEO: Standards-Based Performance* (2005), *Leadership and the Force of Love: Six Keys to Motivating With Love* (2002), and *Professional Standards for the Superintendency*. He has created over 150 scholarly publications over his 40 years in education. He attended Texas A&M on an athletic scholarship and played first base on a conference championship team; he has also served as a public school teacher, coach, and administrator.

Krista Parent is in her eighth year as superintendent for South Lane School District in Oregon. She has been an educator in South Lane for the past 24 years, serving as a teacher, coach, and school administrator. Krista's work as a superintendent has focused on developing a professional learning community in South Lane using the content area of literacy.

Krista was the 2007 National Superintendent of the Year, the first Oregon superintendent to receive the award. She was also named the 2007 Outstanding Young Alumnus for the University of Oregon, an award that was presented to her by University of Oregon President Dave Frohnmayer. Krista received her bachelor's, master's, and doctoral degrees at the University of Oregon and was a student athlete during her undergraduate studies. Krista's dissertation study was about women in the superintendency.

Krista is the chair of the state's "Assessing Leadership Performance" work group. She is also the president of the Oregon Association of School Executives (OASE). Krista is an active member of her community and serves on the local Rotary Board, Chamber of Commerce, Community College Advisory Board, Community Foundation, and Lane Workforce Partnership Board.

In addition to her superintendent hat, Krista is also a mother of two kids, 13 and 9, and coaches a variety of youth sports, depending on the season.

Donald A. Phillips is a former social science teacher who holds a master's degree in education and a doctorate in education, administration, planning, and social policy from Harvard. For the past 7 years, he has served as superintendent of Poway Unified School District, a suburban K–12 school district with over 33,000 students. He has over 18 years of experience as a school district superintendent and has served in the field of education administration for more than 27 years.

Don was recently named 2008 California State Superintendent of the Year by the American Association of School Administrators. He is passionate about public education and has served in leadership roles for many educational organizations, including the Association of California School Administrators, the American Association of School Administrators, the Suburban School Superintendents, and the California School Boards Association. His commitment to continuous learning is reflected in his numerous contributions to publications and workshops at the state and national levels. He has also been active in local chambers of commerce and with the San Diego Junior Achievement organization.

Daniel H. Pink is the author of *A Whole New Mind,* a *New York Times* and *Business Week* bestseller that has been translated into 16 languages, and *Free Agent Nation,* which *Publishers Weekly* says "has become a cornerstone of employee–management relations." Dan's articles on business and technology appear in many publications, including the *New York Times, Harvard Business Review, Fast Company,* and *Wired,* where he is a contributing editor. He also lectures to corporations, associations, and universities in the United States and abroad on economic transformation and the changing world of work. Dan lives in Washington, D.C., with his wife and their three children.

Betty Rosa holds a BA in psychology from the City College of New York, and an MS in education administration and supervision and another MS in education in bilingual education, both from the City University of New York. She also holds an EdM and EdD in administration, planning, and social policy through the Urban Superintendents Program at Harvard University.

Dr. Rosa worked as a bilingual teacher and reading coordinator in the New York City school system and also served as an assistant principal and principal in special education before becoming principal of I.S. 218, a full-service community school in partnership with the Children's Aid Society.

Chancellor Rudy Crew appointed Dr. Rosa to the position of Superintendent of Community School District 8 in the Bronx. One of the schools Dr. Rosa founded, M.S. 101 (Maritime Academy for

Science and Technology), became the number-one middle school in the City of New York based on New York State examination results. Dr. Rosa also served as the Senior Superintendent of the Bronx. She was elected to a 4-year term with the Alumni Council of Harvard's Graduate School of Education and was appointed to a 3-year term with the Principal/Site Administrator Advisory Committee of the American Association of School Administrators. Dr. Rosa has also served as a consulting member of the Educational Research Development Institute.

Dr. Rosa is currently the president of BDJ & J Associates LLC, a company she founded in 2005. BDJ & J serves in a consulting capacity to an array of companies in the educational publishing, software, Internet-based learning, and service fields.

Dr. Rosa serves as a Regent for the State of New York. She is married and has two sons.

Mark J. Stock is an assistant professor of educational leadership at the University of Wyoming. In addition to teaching and writing, he does many workshops and presentations on a variety of topics. He has 19 years of experience as a school administrator, including 11 years as Superintendent of Schools. While Superintendent of Schools, he ran a successful and popular blog site called "The Wawascene" and lived to tell about it. He lives in Laramie, Wyoming, with his wife and their two children.

Dr. Stock says, "It's a blog-eat-blog world, but the tech-savvy superintendent can thrive, not just survive, in today's communication-frenzied world. They used to say you shouldn't argue with those who buy their ink by the barrel, but today everyone has a barrel of ink, so you should probably have one too."

CHAPTER ONE

THE SUPERINTENDENT AS COMMUNICATOR AND DIPLOMAT

PAUL D. HOUSTON

I t is common for school leaders to describe themselves as "CEOs" as they engage in the work of leading very complex organizations. Certainly if you have the responsibility for an organization—whether it's a widget manufacturing operation or the elementary school down the block—you have to have the tools of management, of setting goals, monitoring operations, providing resources, and the like. School districts are not the same as companies however, despite some critics' calls for operating schools more like businesses.

Businesses have the power to control their raw materials. I once worked in a glass factory during college. One of the products was baby food bottles. The company purchasing those bottles randomly inspected each shipment; if one defective or broken bottle was found, the entire trainload was returned to the factory for reinspection and repackaging. Think of that! The next time a parent shows up at the schoolhouse door with a child who has a disability, a learning problem, or even a bad attitude, try sending them back home. Not going to happen. Besides, widgets don't run around individually in

1

all directions ignoring instructions from the plant supervisor. And widgets don't have parents who can sometimes be unreasonable or other times incapable of supporting their little widget. Schools are most definitely not like businesses.

More important is the fact that while school leaders might be responsible, they are not in charge. The transparent nature of public education means that everyone knows what is happening and has the opportunity to weigh in on the subject. When I was a superintendent, I used to joke that I had the easiest job in town because everyone knew how to do it better than I did, and all I needed to do was listen and follow their advice. Of course, I could never get the public to speak with one voice, so it wasn't really that easy.

> *While school leaders might be responsible, they are not in charge. The transparent nature of public education means that everyone knows what is happening and has the opportunity to weigh in on the subject.*

The reality of leading schools and school districts is that everyone went to school, and that very fact leads them to believe they are experts on schools and schooling. Moreover, while accountability in education tends to be centralized, authority is dispersed. When things go wrong in the school system, everyone knows who to call: the superintendent. But the ability to make decisions is spread across the educational landscape. School boards make policy, the federal and state governments mandate outcomes, the courts make orders, the unions create contracts and rules, and the public makes demands and sets expectations. The person at the top finds that the impressive title is merely a target to hang on his or her back while trying to sort out all these competing interests.

As Alan Blankstein, Bob Cole, and I tried to conceptualize this series on *The Soul of Educational Leadership,* I insisted that we consider the unique aspect of educational leadership that requires leaders to lead even when authority and power are not present. For that reason I have always resisted the "CEO" metaphor as a way of describing educational leadership. I just don't think it works. CEOs are in charge; educational leaders can't even make their constituents take a number.

What then is the proper metaphor? I believe it is that of *minister.* Ministerial authority comes from moral authority. Ministers get their power from on high. In the school trade, our moral authority comes from those we work with and the task we have been given.

We work with people's children—their most precious treasures. These newly minted, delicate vessels of possibility are beyond price. They are unique, and each holds a soul that must be tended with care. Even more, they are the future. It is up to the educator to plant the seed and grow the plant into a mighty tree. Our work shapes their future. So holding all that possibility in our care gives us tremendous moral authority.

Beyond that, public education has been tasked with creating the cornerstone of our democracy. Our forefathers envisioned a system of free public education that would create an apprenticeship of liberty—a place where children could learn to be contributors to our democracy. It is not so widely known, however, that the first task of public education originally was not the three R's, but that of creating civic virtue. So educational leaders have all the moral authority they need to do their work.

But the ministerial metaphor goes further. Ministers have no real power beyond their ability to see truth and speak it, to convene folks together and communicate with them. That ability to speak the word and make it flesh lies at the heart of the ministerial role, and I believe it lies at the heart of educational leadership. Educational leaders sit at the crossroads of their communities; they sit at a high place with great perspective. They know what the community is doing or not doing by what happens to the children of that community. Educational leaders see all the pieces of the puzzle. They know the truth—and in knowing it and speaking it, they can set others free.

They also can pull folks together around issues that are important. Presidents of the United States have often been described as having a "bully pulpit." Educational leaders have their own bully pulpit to stand in and be reckoned with. School board meetings, press interviews, civic club speeches, and even the ubiquitous PTA meetings all give the school leader a chance to convene and persuade. And if those opportunities aren't enough, one can always create a task force or special committee to study and report on issues of importance to education.

Convening is no problem. But once convened, then what? This is where persuasion must take place. I believe that the central role of any educational leader is that of communicator. The biggest tool in the leader's box is the ability to

The biggest tool in the leader's box is the ability to communicate clearly and persuasively to the staff, and to the public and policy makers, about what the issues are and how they must be handled.

communicate clearly and persuasively to the staff, and to the public and policy makers, about what the issues are and how they must be handled.

There are certain basic skills that a leader must have: writing, speaking, and perhaps the greatest and most overlooked—listening. Leaders must not only watch their P's and Q's, but they must also dot their I's and cross their T's—literally and figuratively. If you have problems with using the language, educational leadership is not the best role for you. People will read what you write and dissect it. They will listen to what you say and critique it. And they will fully expect you to pay attention to what they tell you and to understand it.

But that's just Communication 101. The real communication skills of an educational leader center on the ability to tell stories and to craft metaphors. Perhaps the greatest communicator in the history of humankind was Jesus Christ. A poor man from humble origins, without resources or power, he has influenced millions of people over thousands of years. Setting aside the question of divinity, Jesus was an incredible communicator. Almost everything he said was a story, a metaphor, or a parable of some sort. He reduced the complexity and often the uncomfortable nature of what he was preaching to words that were accessible to common people.

Far too often, we educators are guilty of using language to obfuscate what we really mean. We use acronyms whose meaning we hardly remember ourselves and expect the layperson to understand what we are talking about. We rattle off statistics without context or reference. For example, it is one thing to say that the war in Iraq will cost America $3 trillion—that is a big and meaningless number. It is another thing to say that those dollars could buy every American man, woman, and child a brand-new car. Now that communicates. We fog up our communications and then we wonder why we don't have the support of the public. Educational leaders need to ban big words and bigger wall charts from their world and start to make things personal and accessible.

I have often urged superintendents to tell their own stories. They should open themselves up and become vulnerable to their communities. That openness will not weaken them—it will give them strength because it will create a powerful bond with those who hear them. The 2008 presidential election has provided new insights into the power of personal story. Barack Obama in particular has shown that the use of personal narrative to tell a larger truth is extremely powerful. On the Republican side, Arkansas Governor Mike

Huckabee came from nowhere to become a serious candidate by using his ability to connect and tell stories that people understood. Ronald Reagan, back in the 1980s, was known as the Great Communicator—a storyteller and a gifted user of language. His famous "Morning in America" speech, made during the 1984 presidential campaign, wasn't just words; it was a vision of hope for a nation. The ability to communicate makes a leader truly a leader.

But words are only part of the story. Researchers tell us that about two-thirds of all communication is nonverbal; it is tone and body language. Further, every educator today knows that there are different learning modalities. Some people learn by hearing or reading, others learn visually, and still others learn tactilely. My point here is that to communicate fully, one must use varied tools. The old saying that a picture is worth a thousand words is true. Effective communicators are able to vary their communications to take a variety of receivers into account.

Beyond using all these tools, a great communicator must also listen. Yogi Berra, the fabled catcher for the New York Yankees, was known for his offbeat phrases that didn't seem to make sense at first but when thought about seemed rather wise. "It ain't over 'til it's over"—while obvious, it states a truth that many overlook as they declare things finished before they really are. Yogi once said that "you can observe a lot just by watching." True. I would add that you can hear a lot just by listening.

But listening is more than just turning on your ears. It's also about turning on your heart. Listening is an act of respect and love for the one you are listening to. You are giving the person your all during that time of hearing him or her out, and you have to listen with a real sense of care and empathy. It isn't about just shutting up and allowing the person to talk, or letting someone get something off his or her chest. You must listen to the person's words, and then listen for what is behind the words. Most of us can't always say what we really mean. Sometimes in very emotional situations we say things in ways that mask or garble what we really want to say. The good communicator uncovers and ungarbles these words by listening with the heart as well as the head.

A couple of years ago, I visited a school district involved in lots of controversy because of squabbles over the use of books in the literature classes that some of the more conservative parents thought should be banned. Other parents wanted the books left in the curriculum. It was a classic case of whose rights get affirmed. As I listened to the parents reading the racier passages from the books and railing at the board and administration for not doing their bidding by immediately removing this material they considered offensive, I found myself setting aside my own anger at these parents who would presume to tell others what their kids could or could not read based on their own values. I found myself hearing what was behind their words: fear. They were trying to bring up their children in a world where they were assaulted on every side by smut and offensive language and ideas, and they wanted to protect them from that. I can't say I think the school should have removed the books just because those parents were offended, but I did find myself wondering about the kind of conversation that could be had if the school took the fear issue seriously and talked with the parents about that.

Albert Einstein said that no problem can be solved at the same level at which it was created. What he meant was that when you see (or hear) a problem, the solution probably lies on a different plane. A controversy about eliminating a class or program in a school is usually rooted in inadequate funding. Sometimes shifting the discussion to a different plane allows communication to flow more easily.

This takes me to the other half of this strangely titled volume: Diplomats. What is a book about school leaders doing talking about being a diplomat? Shouldn't that be in a book about the Foreign Service? No. The need for diplomacy is all around us. We start trying to teach our children at a very early age about the value of diplomacy. The whole lesson of learning to say "please" and "thank you" is really a lesson on diplomacy.

If you have a job with no inherent power, how can you get other folks to do what needs to be done? Diplomacy.

If you have a job with no inherent power, how can you get other folks to do what needs to be done? Diplomacy. In the teachings of Taoism, it is said that a leader should strive to lead in such a way that when the job is done the people say, "We did it ourselves." That seems to me to be at the heart of being a diplomat. It has often been said that there is no job too big to do if people don't care who gets the credit for it. Leading means losing your ego and letting the world flow toward that which must be done. You do that by being a diplomat centered on the outcome, not the process. Diplomacy requires surrendering one's ego for the greater good.

We all know great diplomats when we see them. Many of us were raised by them. All of us have had teachers who were gifted in getting kids to do work that we believed was our own idea. I'm not talking about manipulation here—diplomacy is not about fooling people. It's about respecting them, showing that respect, and working with them toward a better outcome.

Educational leaders have lots of power. Theirs is not conferred power or positional power. It is the inner power created by the ability to rally folks to a cause larger than themselves, to persuade them to do what they know already is the right thing to do, and to do so with a song in their heart. Communication and diplomacy—these are the centerpieces of any leader who leads with a sense of soul and service.

CHAPTER TWO

THE LEADER AS COMMUNICATOR AND DIPLOMAT

KRISTA PARENT

Communication leads to community, that is, to understanding, intimacy, and mutual valuing.

—Rollo May

The world has changed dramatically over the last decade, and the pace of change is likely to intensify. If we are to educate our youth for the uncertain future that is roaring toward us, we must lead in a different way than we have in the past. Our old system has not failed us; it worked well for the era in which it was created. Now, however, it's time to create a new system.

As a school superintendent, I must constantly model and lead learning, and inspire the drive to learn within a school system and community. This requires consistent and clear communication, both internally and externally, as well as a system that makes this a natural part of our work. As a rookie superintendent, I quickly learned that all that goes right and all that goes wrong in a school district ultimately can be traced back to communication—or a lack thereof. Systems must be developed within (and outside) a district to ensure multiple avenues for giving and receiving information, as well as for collaboratively discussing and developing new ideas and initiatives. The ultimate goal of any system of communication is to have many avenues for good information to flow in and out regularly and consistently. In order to inform the communication in a school district, the superintendent must be continuously articulating a vision, thinking, reading, sharing, listening, and reflecting—and then cycling through these processes to better communicate each time.

A national study found that nearly half of all public messages about schools that come from school staff are negative (Banach, 2003). This research suggests that the messengers who provide the most potent and unfavorable influence on the public's perception of schools are not newspapers, television, or even talk radio. They are school employees!

As a rookie superintendent, I quickly learned that all that goes right and all that goes wrong in a school district ultimately can be traced back to communication—or a lack thereof.

> Coupled with decades of research that shows the public trusts school employees as the most credible source of information about schools, our findings lead to the inevitable conclusion that schools need to better inform and engage internal audiences, and that together, we need to communicate more purposefully. (Hawkins, 2006)

DEVELOPING A DISTRICTWIDE COMMUNICATION PLAN

I got my opportunity to develop an internal and external communication system (with a lot of assistance and support) when our district was selected as the state's pilot district for a communication project called "Team Up." Research and collaborative support were made available to us from a range of educational organizations, including the state-level organizations for administrators, school boards, and teachers. All of our schools, departments, and parent clubs participated in the project. The aim of Team Up was to better get the word out (or in some cases "in") about how well our public schools were performing, and to assist school districts statewide to develop effective systems of communication.

Our role as the pilot district was to develop a process that would result in a "playbook" that other districts could use to improve their communication systems. This year-long project began with a thorough examination of our existing internal communication system, including sharing information about how students are performing throughout the district and a survey of all staff members regarding how they felt about the district. Seven brief questions were asked of staff members in departmental or building-level settings to set the stage for sharing state and local data about how well our schools were doing. The seven questions included the following:

1. How was work today?

2. Please tell me one good thing about your school/work.

3. Rate student performance in our district.

4. Rate student performance in our state.

5. How important to student success is parental involvement?

6. How important to student/school success is community involvement?

7. What percentage of school budgets is spent on central administration in our state?

Representatives from the various state educational organizations shared information about general communication, public perceptions, and public school performance across the state. They also interjected local district data (when data were available) for comparative purposes. In addition to realizing that staff members didn't necessarily have accurate information about things like "how much money is spent on administration in your local school district" or "how are our students performing compared to students in neighboring school districts," one of the biggest "aha moments" for staff in our district was how casual conversation with friends or colleagues can easily be misinterpreted. For example, when an acquaintance asks, "How's it going?" while shopping at the local grocery store, and you respond about how difficult things were at school that day— three other shoppers nearby may interpret your message as "things are falling apart in the school district," or "our schools are a really rough place to work."

Our districtwide electronic survey (described further below) made it abundantly clear that staff members felt proud to be a part of the district and had high regard for the work that was being done on behalf of students. Representative comments from the survey are shown below:

- "Strong, cohesive leadership teams that are passionate about their work, enjoy working with one another, and have dedicated their life to education and learning, and literally live each day 'walking the walk' and making it all about the kids!"
- "Student progress is heavily monitored; there are numerous interventions available when students fail; students receive multiple opportunities for success at every level; employees work hard and care about their work."
- "Leadership that works collaboratively with all staff and empowers individuals and individual initiative."

The departmental and school meetings we held as part of Team Up resulted in staff members compiling lists of all the accomplishments they had achieved in the past few years and all the reasons they loved to come to work each day. School and department staffs were eager to share their lists with me and with the larger Team Up Task Force (which included all seven school board members). Staff members also reported feeling more informed about factual data they could use when sharing accomplishments or general information with the community.

We used an electronic survey to get staff feedback on key communication questions and to truly analyze the state of communication within our district. The online survey yielded more than 300 responses from nearly 360 employees. Responses to the survey questions helped form the basis for developing the district's improved communication system. The statewide educational partners developed the survey tool based on their research regarding public school communication over the previous several years. The survey questions were as follows:

Electronic Communication Survey

1. Below are general statements about our schools. Please rate them according to how much you agree or disagree with each statement.

   a. Despite difficult budget circumstances, our schools continue to improve.

   b. Expectations for our students are higher today than they were a generation ago.

   c. Our schools do a good job of keeping employees informed about what is happening in our district.

   d. Our students do better on state reading and math tests than they did 10 years ago.

   e. Most of our parents contribute to the success of their students by being involved in schools.

   f. A lot of community members volunteer in our schools.

   g. Our schools do a good job of keeping the public informed about what is happening in our district.

   h. Our students do better on college entrance tests (such as the SAT) today than they did 10 years ago.

   i. Our students do a lot of volunteer work in the community.

   j. Our schools communicate well with Spanish-speaking parents and community members.

   k. The state and federal standards that our schools are expected to meet are higher today than they were a generation ago.

   l. Our employees are well-informed about the budget and how money is spent.

   m. Most parents check homework and attend parent–teacher conferences.

   n. All things considered, our schools are succeeding.

2. When someone asks about South Lane Schools, the first thing I am likely to tell them is . . .

3. What's the number one reason you think South Lane Schools are succeeding or not succeeding?

4. The following questions are about internal communication and messaging related to our schools. Please rate them according to how much you agree or disagree with each statement.

a. I feel well-informed about what is happening in our schools.
b. What I say to friends and neighbors about our schools influences their opinions about our district.
c. I'd like to know how to debunk some of the negative myths and inaccurate statistics about schools that some people claim are true.
d. As much as possible, I'd like to see us determine clear and effective messages about our schools, and then, together speak with "one voice" in sending them to the public.
e. It isn't part of my job description, but I feel it's part of my responsibility to communicate positively and honestly about our schools.
f. I believe that there is a direct relationship between what employees say outside of work about our schools and the community's perception of our schools—and, as we all know, public perception affects public support for our schools.
g. As long as I know the messages are true and they were developed by a district group that included some of my peers, I am willing to do my best to share recommended messages and stories about our schools with my friends, neighbors, and acquaintances.
h. When I don't agree with a negative comment someone makes about our schools, I'm more likely to ignore it than I am to speak up.
i. When I say things about our schools, people believe I know what I'm talking about.
j. I would have different conversations about our schools with friends and neighbors if I had a clear idea of what messages and stories about our schools would have the greatest positive impact on their perception of schools.

5. I would rate communication within our schools—among staff at all levels, between schools and district, between school/district and parents/community members—as . . .

6. I have the following suggestions for improving communication within the schools . . .

Finally, the survey included a series of nine factual accomplishments about the district; staff members rated whether knowing each of those facts would make a difference in the grade they gave the district. Two examples of the factual accomplishments appear below:

A new superintendent—or any staff member, for that matter—could walk into the district and immediately identify the avenues developed for engaging, ongoing communication.

- If you knew that our district spends less than 4 percent of the budget on central administration, compared to nearly 90 percent in the classroom or on support services for kids such as transportation and food services, would you be more likely to grade our schools higher, grade them lower, or stay the same?
- If you knew that more than 30,000 volunteer hours are donated by parents and community members in our schools each year, would you be more likely to grade our schools higher, grade them lower, or stay the same?

The Team Up process ultimately led to the development of two broad communication goals for the district:

1. Improve the communication system throughout the district to better support student learning.

2. Enhance internal and external perceptions of our schools by focusing communications on the factual successes we are experiencing.

These two goals required staff to support the mission and values of the schools; be committed to the success of schools and students, as well as garnering greater public support for the schools; actively engage in internal and external communication efforts; stay informed about the district's successes and challenges; and understand their own influence when speaking about their local district and about public schools statewide.

The Team Up Task Force was charged with developing a plan for regularly informing citizens in the local community of the district's successes and challenges. The task force formalized an action plan, to be reviewed annually by the school board and district administration, as a guide for the district's ongoing communication efforts. Revisions to the plan have been made as better ways to communicate are shared by both staff and community residents. A new superintendent—or any staff member, for that matter—could walk into the district and immediately identify the avenues developed for engaging, ongoing communication.

LEADERSHIP EXPECTATIONS
FOR COMMUNICATION

As the lead diplomat—ambassador, representative—of my school district, I am charged with making sure that our communication plan is alive and well. Nothing can derail any project or initiative more quickly than misinformation or lack of information. The superintendent must work tirelessly to keep everyone focused on the right things: teaching and learning. Whatever the message, it must tie back to these essentials, because ultimately they are our primary business, our reason for being.

If communication breaks down somewhere in the school system, the superintendent is responsible for adjusting the system or fixing any miscommunications. Our district's leadership team (which includes all district- and school-level administrators, school board members, and preservice administrators) has developed a core set of expectations about how we communicate. We frequently test our message against these expectations to make sure our communication is effective. The five "Leadership Expectations for Communication" include

1. *Transparency.* The message must be crystal clear. The listener/reader should not be left searching for the real message. Communication should be free of educational jargon and acronyms.

2. *Consistent and clear message.* The listener/reader should not receive conflicting communications. The message should be the same regardless of who is responsible for the communication. If someone calls the district office and talks to any of the district administrators, he or she should get the same information or response.

With all communications, stop and ask yourself, "Who else needs to know," before limiting your intended audience.

3. *Compelling and factual stories.* Stories should focus on student, staff, and school/district success. Information must always be accurate and factual.

4. *Humor.* A sense of humor is critical to getting along in today's world. Appropriate humor is a useful way of engaging the listener. Humor must be used carefully, however—depending on the subject and the audience, humor may not always be the best approach.

5. *Always asking who needs to know.* It is imperative to get the information to those who need to know it. With all communications, stop and ask yourself, "Who else needs to know," before limiting your intended audience.

INNOVATIVE STRATEGIES FOR ENCOURAGING COMMUNICATION

In addition to ensuring that our formal communication plan is working, I'm always seeking innovative, compelling strategies for encouraging individuals to engage in communication that has the power to improve learning for all students. This requires a certain amount of creativity on the part of the superintendent, as well as learning from other great communicators about their strategies and then adapting them to fit one's own local situation. Five strategies that have proven to be effective in our district are the following:

1. **Forums** to openly share thoughts and ideas with district administration and school board members. We've titled these forums "Banter with the Boss." Employees from the entire district are invited to the central office to share their thoughts on a variety of topics, such as

   - Five years from now I hope our district will . . .
   - The stupidest thing our district does is . . .
   - What could the district do to change your response to the previous question?
   - The one thing the district could do to make me more effective in my role is . . .
   - Kids in this district would be better served if only the district would . . .
   - My biggest peeve with the district administration/school board is . . .
   - The one area I feel really in the dark about and about which I would like the district to share more information is . . .

The questions are intentionally candid and invite constructive criticism. You have to be prepared to really listen to responses with an open mind. This strategy demonstrates your willingness as a leader to talk about the hard things and to make changes when they are necessary. Such forums also have the power to create a culture honoring the reality that we all have room for improvement and need to be continuous learners. It is important, incidentally, for the superintendent to prepare central office administrators and school board members if they are to be included in this format. These forums are no place for being defensive or taking things personally.

This may not be a strategy for a new superintendent to use immediately, because a trusting relationship must first be established so that staff members feel comfortable speaking candidly and freely. I began using this strategy in my second year as superintendent, but I had been in the district 18 years at that point; everyone knew what I stood for, and I had developed people's confidence that this was a safe activity to engage in. I recommend modifying this strategy—by designing questions that are less intense, for example—if you're still working to establish this kind of atmosphere.

2. **Weekly electronic e-mails** to all district employees and the community describing something great that's happening in the district and providing contact information. The title of these weekly e-mails is "What's Right in XXX School District." These messages are generally four to five sentences about an important success that individuals might not necessarily hear about in the general media. An example of a "What's Right?" message might be the one below:

> In partnership with the local Rotary Club, more than 100 computers are being given away to middle and high school students participating in the district's after-school program. Training is provided to students and families before they take their new computer home and includes basic setup practice, troubleshooting tips, and how to access educational resources. For more information, contact Mr. Joe Smith [include contact phone number and e-mail].

3. **A district and community task force focused on "Schools of the Future."** In our district, approximately 100 participants come together three to four times a year to think and talk about our students' future. This work engages our school board members in a communitywide conversation looking at future trends affecting education and the economy, and then developing a vision of where we want student learning to be in 5 to 10 years. Task force participants address a series of such questions as, "If you were king or queen for a day, what would you implement or change?" Subcommittees were formed around five themes that emerged from the large-group discussions.

4. **A monthly electronic newsletter** with well-written stories about school district projects and opportunities. Numerous links are embedded within the newsletter to provide in-depth information for those interested in exploring a particular topic in more detail. We are currently working to provide links to both podcasts and video footage of professional development activities throughout the district.

5. **Regular columns and guest editorials in** the local newspaper about a variety of topics. In smaller communities, this is fairly easy to accomplish because the local newspaper needs contributions to keep the public well-informed. I generally keep a running list of ideas for guest columns; I even write some of them ahead of time and submit them whenever it seems appropriate. It is important for leaders to have a finger on the pulse of the community in order to know what topics are likely to be timely. Enlisting other administrators and school board members to contribute in their areas of expertise is also helpful.

It doesn't help to have a central office team that agrees with everything you suggest. If this is the case, you are likely missing the mark on most of your communications.

These five strategies have become a mainstay of our district's communication plan. Staff and community members rely on this information and frequently report feeling better informed because of these tools. Listening to both formal and informal conversations in the district—and in our local community—is a helpful way of focusing the topics for each of the strategies above.

Personal note: As superintendent, it's important for you to have a colleague in the central office who can be relied upon to be open and honest about what he or she is hearing in the community—and to be willing to refocus your thinking if you get off track. It doesn't help to have a central office team that agrees with everything you suggest. If this is the case, you are likely missing the mark on most of your communications.

Outside of the district's formal communication plan—but equally important—is the superintendent's critical role in developing and maintaining positive relationships with staff, community citizens, parents, and students. The superintendent is always representing the school district, 24/7, even when playing other roles simultaneously—parent, neighbor, youth coach, or service club member, for instance. No amount of technological pizzazz can substitute for face-to-face time spent with any group of stakeholders. The superintendent must be seen as highly competent, credible, and visible. He or she must be a regular classroom observer, a spectator at extracurricular activities, and a leader of professional development. The words and actions of the superintendent must convey fairness, passion, and a vision for what is best for students.

Being the ambassador for the school district also means being the public servant, public relations expert, moderator, mediator, negotiator, and peacekeeper. Your eyes and ears must be wide open at all times to stay in touch with the needs of your staff and community.

Finally, the superintendent must be *trusted.* In the absence of trust, it is difficult (and maybe impossible) to achieve effective communication. According to Stephen Covey in *The Speed of Trust* (2006), the two critical factors in trust are character and competence. Both are necessary attributes of a leader—*any* leader. If either one is lacking, there will be a deficit in trust, and then communication is likely to break down.

SUPERINTENDENT AND SCHOOL BOARD COMMUNICATION

I would be remiss if I didn't discuss the critical role of communication between the superintendent and school board in ensuring an aligned communication. This may be one of the most difficult tasks that face any superintendent. If it is done poorly, the rest of the communication system—indeed, the superintendent's vision for the whole district—can be undermined.

I believe that, for rookie superintendents, the matter of board–superintendent relations may be one of the biggest surprises of the job. Knowing your school board members and their individual needs regarding communication is essential to making the whole system work smoothly. For some board members, it is necessary to "overcommunicate." Other board members may want to know only the basics. Understanding board members' individual needs is an important way in which superintendents can keep board members in tune with district plans and initiatives and help everyone stay informed.

I've seen too many superintendents work terribly hard to develop a community of learners, only to leave their school board members out of the process. Some school boards are reluctant to become deeply involved in instructional matters; these boards tend to focus more on operational matters such as facilities or the budget. If we are truly going to transform the way we educate our students, however, school board members must become involved in student learning. This is not always an easy task, but a clever superintendent can figure out ways to engage board members in this vitally important work.

One way we've accomplished this is to use a book club format to engage school board members in discussions with district staff about how to improve student academic performance and success for all. We have devoted several board work sessions each year to discussing strategic topics in greater depth. We constantly share our new learnings with board members and are now able to engage them in that learning as well.

A critical component of a good communication system is developing ways to "invite" others into the conversation. If you sit back and wait for others to share their thoughts and ideas, your system will not be effective. In regard to the school board, I've found that inviting them to read leadership and instructional materials, right along with our staff, helps them become engaged in important conversations about improved learning for all. Reading the same materials together, and then discussing the ideas we've read, levels the playing field for all to participate in discussions and planning. We've even used this format with community members in our "Schools for the Future" Task Force. This format is a nonthreatening way for all—educators and patrons alike—to engage in critical discussions about how to improve student academic performance.

Our most recent attempt at inviting the school board into the conversation was to ask each administrator and board member to read at least one of five books focused on the future. They chose from the following five selections:

- *A Whole New Mind,* Daniel Pink (2006)
- *The Medici Effect,* Frans Johansson (2006)
- *Crash Course,* Chris Whittle (2005)
- *Future-Focused Leadership,* Gary Marx (2006)
- *Sixteen Trends,* Gary Marx (2006)

In preparation for facilitated discussions about the readings, all participants were asked to come prepared to share three major insights or interesting ideas they found in the reading, two ideas that made them question something we were currently doing in our schools, and one idea they would like to pursue in more detail. During a 5-hour work session, school board members and administrators shared their thinking with others who had read the same book, then shared the critical learning with the whole group. The thoughtful, provocative communication allowed a wide range of perspectives to be heard by a fairly large group. The work session concluded with conversation about the following questions:

- How should our new learning affect the vision we have for our students? What does this mean personally for you in the role that you play in the district?
- How do these ideas get represented in the school board goals, district improvement plan goals, and strategic portfolio list?
- What are the implications if we were to implement some of these ideas? What are the barriers we might face?

Finally, each group presented its thoughts on the above questions and suggested ideas for the district's strategic portfolio list. This approach entails what Doug Eadie (2005) refers to as "above-the-line" change initiatives that are developed to address high-priority issues that can't afford to become buried in a lengthy, long-term plan. These ideas are generally "out-of-the-box" innovations that aren't a part of the operational planning. Once such projects are implemented, they're removed from the list. We had introduced our school board to Eadie's idea of a "strategic change portfolio" approach to planning, as opposed to a more traditional strategic plan; Eadie's approach has helped our board members become more involved as part of the learning community. We've found the strategic portfolio approach to be more responsive and engaging, especially considering the fast-changing times in which we're living.

CONCLUSION

Developing a dynamic, effective communication system for a school district requires careful thought, creativity, and planning. As the "ambassador" for the school district, the superintendent should be

If your communication system is a "reactive" one, it is time to rethink your plan.

the hub of this system, regardless of the size of the district. It is the superintendent's role to communicate in a way that unites everyone in the system around a common vision for students. The communication system must allow for information to be shared in a variety of formats and in multiple directions. If your communication system is a "reactive" one, it is time to rethink your plan. Communication should be forward-thinking, anticipating the needs of the district's stakeholders before they are even aware of those needs.

Among the basics regarding communication, superintendents should include the need to develop a relationship with all media contacts so that they know they can count on you for the factual information they seek. Regular meeting time spent with your media contacts before "big stories" occur will pay off tremendously in the long run and will help the media folks feel prepared and knowledgeable when the news stories break. Making yourself available—not just to the media, but to a variety of in-district and community groups—should be a part of your communication plan. Plenty of good resources are readily available to help leaders navigate the "dos and don'ts" of communication. In this day and age, it is essential to use technology to enhance the district's communication system. If you are a superintendent who doesn't know how technology can support your communication system, now is the time to learn. The proper technology properly used can make a complex system very doable.

Communication is ultimately the way in which a superintendent will get things accomplished—whether it is professional development efforts, high school closings or reorganizations, annual budgeting, or facilities planning. In order to ensure that everyone in the system is learning—and this certainly includes adults as well as students—the superintendent must know what's on the horizon by reading, learning, listening, and scanning the environment, and then using the communication system to share ideas, get feedback, and take action. In a school district where all students are experiencing success, you are likely to find a communication system that is working smoothly.

REFERENCES

Banach, W. J. (2003, Summer). What students, parents, and staff are saying about schools. *Journal of School Public Relations, 24*(3), 187–198.

Covey, S. M. R. (2006). *The speed of trust.* New York: Free Press.

Eadie, D. (2005). *Five habits of high-impact school boards.* Lanham, MD: Scarecrow Education.

Hawkins, C. (2006). *Team Up planning process.* Salem, OR: Confederation of Oregon School Administrators.

CHAPTER THREE

THE EDUCATIONAL LEADER

*Diplomat and Communicator
for All Students*

JOHN R. HOYLE

John Sanders was in his first year as assistant principal at a middle school in a West Texas city after serving as a head baseball coach at the local high school. Sanders, who had recently completed both his master's degree and administrator certification, had been selected by the superintendent to fill the position at a middle school in the poorest part of the city. Over 60 percent of the students were either first- or second-generation Mexican Americans. Approximately 40 percent of the students spoke Spanish at home; many had difficulty speaking, reading, and writing English. Only 5 of the 35 teachers in the middle school could speak or read Spanish, and most knew very little about the community.

Sanders himself knew very little about the local Mexican American culture and could speak only a few words of Spanish. He had an advantage over the teachers, however, because he had played on the local League of Unified Latin American Citizens (LULAC) baseball team the previous summer. Sanders' friend Roy Marin, a well-known Hispanic high school administrator, had introduced Sanders to members of the local LULAC team and invited him to play first base. The baseball games were a big Sunday afternoon social event for the Hispanic community, with Mexican food, music, and plenty of ice-cold, locally brewed beer. Sanders also did some pitching when Marin needed relief during the hot Sunday afternoon games. The only European Americans in the ballpark, Sanders and his wife easily stood out in the crowd.

While Sanders struggled to balance his roles as disciplinarian, teacher supervisor, and coordinator of in-school and after-school events, he continued to treat each parent and student with diplomacy and respect.

John Sanders quickly became a diplomat for the school and the primary communicator about school issues with the Hispanic families. This close relationship helped ease his transition from high school teaching to his new role as assistant principal with responsibilities for school discipline and attendance monitoring. Most of the Hispanic students knew Sanders as a LULAC baseball player and greeted him with a smile each school day. Sanders' boss, an experienced principal, told him to be cautious about getting "too close to these Mexican kids because some cannot be trusted." He told Sanders to keep a tight rein on them and even to use the paddle on the worst ones in order to keep the others in line. While Sanders struggled to balance his roles as disciplinarian, teacher supervisor, and coordinator of in-school and after-school events, he continued to treat each parent and student with diplomacy and respect. Acts of diplomacy toward these families by the school principals and staff had been rare before Sanders. In fact, some hostility existed between the Hispanic community and the school district.

Sanders was invited to be the featured speaker at the LULAC baseball banquet, which honored all baseball players from Little League to the men's team. After the banquet, several of his teammates (and fathers of his students) informed him that they would need to pull their children out of school for a period of 4 to 6 weeks to work with their families as fruit pickers in Michigan. The fathers told Sanders that they needed the money to survive and pay rent. They asked Sanders if their children would fail a grade for missing so much school and become dropouts like themselves.

Sanders made no promises but told the fathers and mothers that he would see what he could do and get back to them. He drew on his best diplomatic skills as he discussed the plight of the students from migrant families with his principal and with others downtown in the central office. He asked if this situation had arisen before and if there was any flexibility in the attendance rules. He was told, "Unless there has been some kind of home-schooling arrangement, if they have more than 20 unexcused school days we require them to repeat the grade. They cost us state attendance money when they follow the harvest each fall." Sanders was unhappy with the answers, but he thanked his superiors for their time and consideration for his students.

At this point, Sanders faced a difficult moral dilemma about whether to consider bending the rules to help these Hispanic students succeed in school. He reasoned that state school attendance laws had been designed for the right reasons—to seek adequate funding and accurate accounting for school attendance. However, Sanders believed that the rules were inflexible and unfair for these students; he began thinking of ways to bend them that would help to change a long-term pattern of failure for poor Hispanic students. Existing policies made no exceptions for children of families that were forced to follow jobs for their survival.

Sanders spoke with the students who would accompany their families in following the harvest and told them that they must be counted absent because of state attendance laws, but that he would talk to their teachers about keeping them on their class rolls during their time away. Sanders then used his communication and persuasion skills to appeal to each of the students' teachers. He was pleasantly surprised that each teacher agreed to keep the students on their class rolls, as long as it was not against the law. Sanders assured them that if any laws were violated, he would assume full responsibility. He diplomatically thanked them for their concern and extra work in helping these children face this difficult situation. Sanders then persuaded the teachers to help him supply the students with textbooks and worksheets, as well as the class assignments, during their extended absences.

The last step was calling a meeting for the Hispanic parents and students at the LULAC building several days before they left for work in Michigan, Indiana, and Illinois. He informed them about the teachers' willingness to help their children by supplying school assignments, books, and worksheets for the 4- to 6-week absences. He urged the students to read the books and complete each worksheet so that they could keep up with their classmates back home. Sanders asked the parents to assure him that the material would be returned in good shape and that their sons and daughters would be allowed study time each evening after the long workday. The parents agreed to do the best they could under the circumstances and thanked Sanders for his help. Within 3 days, approximately 25 students left with their families on the journey north.

Did Sanders' attempts at diplomacy go too far in asking teachers to bend the rules? Was he right in asking them to keep the absent migrant students on class rolls and to lend them state-owned books, school district worksheets, and other materials? Why did Sanders decide to put certain students first and apply his skills of diplomacy and persuasion to help these students and challenge current practice—when it would have been much easier and safer to carry out his duties as assigned? After all, schools are conservative entities that tend to promote upwardly mobile school administrators who play by all the rules and act as loyal team players.

Sanders had been taught by his professor and advisor in graduate school to obey existing laws and policies, but always to put the welfare of students first. While Sanders had a personal goal of becoming a school superintendent or university professor, he also had a philosophy of life that included challenging unjust systems. Deep in his soul, he knew that what occurred each year in his school was unjust, but over time it had become acceptable practice to policy makers and school officials. Sanders struggled with moral conflicts between following the current practice, which acted to push migrant children out of the system, and bending the rules to help them succeed scholastically.

> *Deep in his soul, he knew that what occurred each year in his school was unjust, but over time it had become acceptable practice to policy makers and school officials.*

The psychologist Thomas Moore (1992) would have understood Sanders' moral dilemma because he believes that leaders must include spirituality to nurture the soul in guiding both behavior and difficult personal decisions. Sanders, well-educated and employed at the upper levels of the socioeconomic scale, was growing closer to poor people from a different culture. He was deeply concerned that these less-privileged children under his care were doomed to failure unless he used his skills as a communicator and diplomat to influence the process with which they were struggling. He knew that the school system was controlled by politicians and educators whose efforts were focused on greater rigor in math and science, improved teacher and administrator preparation, longer school years, and more "high stakes" testing in order to compete globally. Sanders was deeply troubled that the No Child Left Behind Act (NCLB) and related politico-corporate–driven legislation were not designed to help children with the greatest social and learning deficits. He took professional risks in trying to convince others that the laws were unjust and that an increased range of means for evaluating student success was needed more urgently than ever. He reminded his superiors and teachers that under the existing model, over half of the Hispanic students who graduated from his middle school would never earn a high school diploma because many of them would never reach tenth grade.

Moore (1992) agrees with many school leaders that when any child is left behind based on a single test score, alternative measures must be applied if social justice is to prevail in America. Moore believes that the current narrow system of accountability used to assess the worthiness of all students, based on America's drive for efficiency in maintaining the world's highest gross national product, is misguided and damages the human soul. He writes, "The United States ranks low on the list of how well nations take care of their children. . . . If we were really to care for the child, we would have to face our own lower natures—our indomitable emotions, our insane desires, and the vast range of our incapacity" (p. 53). Thus the criteria used in high-stakes testing tend to promote our lower natures—driving masses of impoverished children out of the system and damaging our souls.

Sanders grew up in a middle-class suburban neighborhood and attended a high school with mostly European Americans and about 10 percent second-generation Mexican Americans. He was an accomplished athlete in three sports and played with three Mexican Americans on his high school baseball team. After playing college baseball and briefly attempting a professional athletic career, Sanders then became a high school baseball coach before assuming his new administrative role at the middle school.

Now, faced with students whose primary language is not English and who have little hope for an educated life, Sanders was beginning his spiritual journey as a person and a school administrator in a new environment. He began to seek a higher vision of service that required him to search his innermost being about ways of using his education, diplomacy, and communication skills to help students on the lower level of society's hierarchy overcome impossible odds and succeed in life.

Preparing Diplomatic School Leaders

How do university programs of leadership preparation, as well as professional administrator associations, teach school leaders to lead with soul and to apply diplomatic skills in persuading others within the educational system that students come first? Since the 1920s, graduate programs in school administration have acknowledged the need to select candidates and prepare them to be community leaders as a means of helping to create democratic schools for all students.

In 1933, Willard Waller, a professor at the University of Chicago, claimed that school leaders are viewed as paragons of virtue, possessing correct values that correspond to those of the communities in which they live and serve. How do leaders continue to be "paragons of virtue" in today's world of political conflict, high-stakes testing, and limited funding? How do they diplomatically convince others that several national and state accountability mandates have proven to be unfair for many poor students from different cultures and ethnicities?

Professional behavior means modeling integrity, sincerity, truthfulness, and honesty. Possessing a code of conduct is one thing; living it is quite another.

How do school administrators learn to be sensitive to the values of one ethnic group without offending the sensibilities of another? How do they know when the "right" set of professional values and ethics is being communicated or followed?

Professional behavior means modeling integrity, sincerity, truthfulness, and honesty. Possessing a code of conduct is one thing; living it is quite another. For today's school leaders who are attempting to meet the needs of a diverse and demanding society, codes of ethics and morals for decision making should not be carved in stone, in perpetuity. Ethical leaders must be developed who can follow laws, policies, and codes of conduct—but who also know when and where to persuade others that rules must be changed or bent for students if the "Generic Kid" is to find success in our society.

Sanders frequently stated that his wish for all his students was simple: "I want each of these students to be as happy and fulfilled as

I am when they reach my age." He occasionally reminded others about a song dealing with racism from the musical *South Pacific:* "You've Got to Be Carefully Taught." His message here was that we *learn* forms of racism, bigotry, and ways of gaining advantage over "those people" from our families, some teachers, some administrators, some coaches, or some ministers, and from school and university systems that were created to exclude rather than include some students. We observe occasional unfair, unethical practices by our politicians, entertainers, athletes, and corporate executives and end up concluding that most of our role models either do not tell the truth or cheat the system.

Recent studies note that over 75 percent of all high school and college students admit to cheating at least once in order to gain a competitive advantage. In their compelling book *Collateral Damage,* Sharon Nichols and David Berliner (2007) report that cheating in school seems to be an integral offshoot of the high-stakes testing movement. A principal in Camden, New Jersey, was dismissed after claiming that he had been pressured by a district official to alter students' answers on the state high school proficiency exam. Another teacher was forced out of a school for blowing the whistle on other teachers who provided correct answers to their students during testing.

Have we created an accountability system that forces us to break the law in trying to make our schools and ourselves appear to be successful? Nichols and Berliner (2007) are convincing when they claim that the high-stakes tests required by NCLB to measure student achievement are wrong-headed. They support their claim by including Donald Campbell's law that declares that the application of any single quantitative social indicator used for social decision making is subject to corruption pressures and is likely to create corruption in the social processes it was intended to measure. Thus the use of a single test score to determine a child's future is a misguided practice that troubles the soul of most school leaders in America.

However, I did not write this chapter to explore the merits of social decision making or to debate the merits of high-stakes testing, but to discuss the means of preparing and developing school leaders who possess skills of communication and diplomacy. These skills are mandatory for principals and superintendents if they are to speak out for those who cannot speak for themselves. We need school leaders with the diplomatic and communication skills to influence change in bureaucratic rules that may impede a child from succeeding in our educational system. Preparing diplomatic, articulate leaders implies that they will go on to use their abilities to speak out against injustice and in some cases jeopardize their careers. Pushing to change these entrenched rules has increased the number of U-Haul trucks being driven by courageous former superintendents.

Teaching prospective school administrators to communicate from the soul is a never-ending task. Books by Tom Sergiovanni, Terry Deal, Michael Fullan, Paul Houston, and this writer explore the depths of the soul and ways of creating learning communities that express unconditional love and interpersonal sensitivity. Despite these writings, research is practically silent on workable strategies for speaking out against injustice and challenging current archaic state and national rules for student assessment.

Most observers of school reform know that a successful school has strong, positive, and healthy teacher–principal relationships. This positive, healthy relationship is considerably damaged as a result of excessive pressure on the school to increase high-stakes test scores. Throw in the controversial practice of linking merit or incentive pay to higher scores, and morale can plummet.

However, preparing and developing school administrators who care about the life struggles of others and providing them with the best skills in diplomacy and communication continue to perplex scholars and practitioners alike. It is important that both school administrators and their professors model interpersonal sensitivity while using diplomacy to communicate with legislators, school board members, and voters about the best practices in teaching and the assessment of all students. Unless teachers, staff, and students sense that the principal or superintendent cares first about their needs and their concerns, very little progress will be made toward empowering others. Certainly, in the story that opened this chapter, John Sanders applied his skills in diplomacy and communication to challenge the rules and help the Hispanic students under his care. To select and prepare leaders like Sanders who have the character, skills, knowledge, compassion, and courage for leading with love, soul, and heart, I suggest the following:

1. Select selfless, articulate, diplomatic candidates for leadership preparation.

2. Assign aspiring school administrators to community agencies.

3. Require conflict resolution training for future and current school leaders.

1. Select selfless, articulate, diplomatic candidates for leadership preparation. The characteristics for leading with soul and love are agreed upon by most observers: caring, respect for self and others, a spirit of forgiveness, selflessness, ethics, enthusiasm, and vision. These are among the characteristics found in the best school leaders. However, it is difficult to predict which candidates will have the courage to challenge injustice and communicate those challenges in a diplomatic manner.

America definitely needs school leaders with heart and soul, but leaders also need skills in communicating and influencing policy makers about necessary changes in school policy to promote equity and justice for all children.

America definitely needs school leaders with heart and soul, but leaders also need skills in communicating and influencing policy makers about necessary changes in school policy to promote equity and justice for all children. We need candidates who are guided by selfless, spiritual gifts who can communicate these traits in influencing policy makers. Spiritualist Deepak Chopra (2002) advises us to select future leaders who grow from the inside out. This spiritual dimension of leadership will help to create a learning community that makes every attempt to adjust the system to assure that all children become successful, ethical individuals. To lack the capacity to care about a child's failure in school or to ignore students' background or family circumstance is *spiritless* leadership. The following two individuals represent the kind of individuals needed in school administration. When I seek candidates for graduate programs, I seek the human attributes found in Jess and Laura.

Jess is a fun-loving, respectful, bright, and very sensitive young man who is an ideal candidate for graduate study in school leadership. Since his childhood, Jess has been kind and thoughtful of the needs of others—except when playing left offensive tackle on his high school football team. He and two others on the team were the spiritual glue that held the team together through the long, hot drudgery of August practices, injuries to key players, and early losses to inferior teams. During these difficult times, Jess rarely griped about practice but became the team diplomat with the coaches, as well as the cheerleader who urged his teammates to work harder and have fun despite the suffering under demanding coaches. His communication skills boosted the morale in the dressing room and on the playing field.

Jess was friendly and respectful to all his classmates in the hallways and on the field. He never sought the limelight but always bragged about his teammates, the team managers, and the coaches—and he diplomatically congratulated members of the opposing team. It was evident to close observers of Jess's team that they had few if any stars, but they kept winning. They went all the way to the state semifinals before losing to the eventual state champion. Jess was not a regular starter, but without his leadership and pass blocking, the team would not have been as successful.

Jess's finest attribute was his integrity. Soon after his senior English teacher handed out a midterm exam, Jess found an answer code in the third page of his test. Immediately he told his teacher about her mistake; she had inadvertently left the answer key in the exam she handed to Jess. Recognized for his act of honesty by the principal, Jess responded, "Anyone would have done the same thing."

After Jess graduates from college, I will follow his teaching career and hope to recruit him into our leadership education program. His strong interpersonal skills, diplomacy, moral center, intellect, and enthusiasm are a solid foundation on which the knowledge base of educational administration can rest.

The second individual, Laura, is truly a servant-leader teacher. She is a selfless, caring person with the spiritual center and communication skills that school leaders need. Whenever a job is to be done, a person needs help, or an errand needs to be run, Laura steps up. In conversation, it is never about her but about you.

While Laura herself has many talents, she is always focused on the talents and accomplishments of others. She has a friend who underwent extensive cancer treatment in a clinic 90 miles away. On several days, Laura picked up her friend and drove him to his radiation treatments on the 180-mile round trip. She visited him and others she knew (and some she did not know) in hospitals and assisted living centers. This intelligent, sensitive, tireless servant-leader bears other people's pain and makes their lives richer. Her sense of humor helps individuals through difficult times. She has the characteristics necessary for leading with soul that all school leaders need. When a child is having learning or disciplinary problems, the principal asks Laura if she will add him or her to her class. In several student assessment issues faced by Laura and her colleagues, Laura became the unofficial spokesperson with the building principal and the district testing administrator. In each case, she used her skills in diplomacy and communication to help overturn decisions to retain some students. The administrators knew that Laura's motive was to help the child become a better student and person. In time, if Laura chooses to leave the middle school classroom and seek a career in school administration, she can be sure of finding a place in any leadership education program. She has the leadership soul on which any other skills can be built.

Degree and licensure programs in educational leadership teach valuable courses on the sociological, historical, and psychological issues of racism, gender, religion, and poverty that will add to the knowledge base and compassion of candidates like Jess and Laura. We also teach AASA/ISLLC-grounded standards that include skills in visioning; creating a school culture for all students; and ensuring resources for a safe, efficient learning environment. Future administrators learn to build collaborative learning communities; act with integrity—fairly and ethically; and grasp the complexities of the political, social, economic, and legal issues.

A preeminently important task for professors in programs of leadership education is first to recruit individuals who lead with soul and have a record of success in various leadership capacities, and then to teach these individuals the skills to manage effective schools and school districts.

A preeminently important task for professors in programs of leadership education is first to recruit individuals who lead with soul and have a record of success in various leadership capacities, and then to teach these individuals the skills to manage effective schools and school districts. One major gap in most programs of preparation and professional development is the teaching of skills in diplomacy and persuasion. These skills can be greatly enhanced by simulating presentations to school boards, the legislature, or community groups that focus on controversial school policies. Moreover, such simulations could include debates on issues of norm- and criterion-referenced testing; bilingual education; authentic performance assessment alternatives; merit pay for higher-performing schools; and, of course, NCLB and state accountability.

The best talent scouts for the tricky process of identifying articulate, diplomatic future school administrators are school principals, superintendents, classroom teachers, counselors, coaches, and graduate and undergraduate professors. Observing the behavior and communication skills of colleagues on a daily basis is a stronger predictor of success than the admissions processes of many graduate programs. Collaboration between professors and school leaders in selecting master's and doctoral-level cohorts of 10 to 20 students is proving to be the best selection model. The school administrators and teacher leadership teams recommend top candidates with the "right stuff," and the university faculty determines if each candidate qualifies academically.

This collaborative process works very well to select the best candidates for degree and licensure programs. If a potential student has a sterling academic record and scores at the upper limits of the Graduate Records Exam, but lacks the soul of leadership or the "fire in the belly" to lead, he or she should be denied admission. Some professors may guide bright candidates with no interest in becoming school administrators into higher education to become researchers or university professors. These young scholars might earn tenure and promotion due to their scholarly productivity, but if they have little or no experience in schools, they often carry scant positive influence with students in their classes or provide little encouragement for their students to become public school administrators.

Leadership education programs continue to cope with the tensions between teaching and mentoring future school administrators, and meeting the tenure/promotion requirements for career advancement. Both roles must be kept in perspective, but selecting and preparing future servant-leaders in graduate programs is of the utmost importance. If these graduates choose to enter higher education at a later date, they will possess the skills of diplomacy and communication necessary to prepare them for both higher education and public school leadership.

2. Assign aspiring school administrators to community agencies. Newly recruited servant-leaders should be assigned to spend time in community agencies that serve the poor, homeless, and aging populations. Since most graduate courses require 45 hours of class content time per semester, I would allocate at least 15 hours of that time for observation in these agencies. For instance, if an urban community has a Boys or Girls Club, the student could spend 3 hours during the first week learning from the directors and volunteers. A second week could be spent in a homeless shelter or shelter for abused persons, the Salvation Army, or a medical clinic for indigent persons. The other hours might be spent on the line at a food kitchen or serving food to elderly people in an assisted living center.

In another class—possibly one focusing on issues of race or urban schools—the student could spend time in the immediate school neighborhood, talking to students and guardians about community safety, drug-related problems, and the school the children attend. Another valuable experience would be with law enforcement agencies to discover what kind of youth sports activities, mentoring, and other programs are being used to help fight vandalism, crime, and the dropout rate.

Professors must reach out to establish positive contacts with key personnel in such agencies to build trust and open communications. Some of these student assignments could be in politically sensitive areas or programs. Trust and integrity must be maintained in order to keep these kinds of valuable opportunities available for future aspiring school leaders. These real-world experiences in agencies and communities could be a superior means of helping to build skills in diplomacy and interpersonal sensitivity the students need—and they could also be quite relevant to formal class work. Leaders with servant souls must be selected and provided with opportunities to learn diplomacy and skills in communicating the needs created by the real world of poverty and racism.

3. Provide conflict resolution training to future and current school administrators. Organizational conflict occurs when two or more individuals differ about how things should be done. Observers of conflict believe that difficulties created by change in organizations and miscommunication of ideas are the sources of most conflicts. When mechanisms exist to help process individual and group conflict, individuals can seek their highest good and progress can be made.

Conflict can lead to destruction of organizational morale, or it can promote *con*struction by allowing the sharing of ideas about ways of improving the organization and establishing a new shared vision. A wise observer of school organizations said that managing conflict in schools is similar to creating pearls. A little grit, managed appropriately, can produce a smoother operating organization or a beautiful pearl! According to Robert Owens and Tom Valesky (2007), conflict is triggered by one individual's frustration with the acts of another, and that unless a process of conflict resolution exists, conflict can lead to hostility

Conflict can lead to destruction of organizational morale, or it can promote construction by allowing the sharing of ideas about ways of improving the organization and establishing a new shared vision.

and ugly confrontations. These confrontations can devastate an organization's morale. Without conflict, however, no organization can continue to improve its effectiveness.

Most writers on organizational conflict recognize the seminal work of Kenneth Thomas (1976) and his useful typology for examining five conflict management styles: competing, collaborating, compromising, avoiding, and accommodating. School administrators often need to *compete* with others for supplies or for new staff. They must *collaborate* to solve school problems or change school operations that may require bending some rules. They must learn to *compromise* with central office administrators in order to adjust programs or classes to help each child succeed, and work with parents, staff, and teachers to seek the best solutions to help all students. There are times and situations for *avoiding* certain conflicts if alternative solutions are anticipated. Also, according to Thomas, knowing when and how to *accommodate* others to ameliorate conflict is good leadership.

Observers of organizational conflict recognize that each of Thomas's five styles can assist school administrators in identifying and avoiding conflicts between individuals and groups when attempting to satisfy individual and organizational needs. Individual employees' needs are typically in constant friction with numerous organizational demands or goals. This conflict was graphically displayed by Jacob Getzels in his *social systems model* over 50 years ago. Getzels hypothesized that three types of conflicts can be found in organizations: role conflict, personality conflict, and role-personality conflict. Getzels found a natural incongruence between organizational goals and individuals' personalities and needs. According to Dan Griffiths (1964), in Getzel's social systems model this incongruence is symptomatic of administrative failure and leads to loss for both the individual and the organization. Many years later, the quality guru W. Edwards Deming concurred with Getzels that conflicts between managerial processes created by excessive demands for higher productivity and ignoring the needs and feedback from the workers lead to poor quality and unhappy customers. It is very important that both aspiring and current school administrators have a strong theory base in order to anticipate and manage organizational conflict.

Perhaps the most devastating outcome of conflict is when irreparable damage is done to a shared organizational vision. When shared visions in a school are shattered by out-of-control egos, individuals, or groups trying to control resources and dominate the ideas of others, conflict can be a permanent condition.

Conflict can be constructive if it is managed properly, however. The spiritual leader should use every means possible to avoid a win–lose conflict situation. In win–lose situations, the school or school district has lost ground in creating collaborative learning communities. When budget, curriculum, or instructional decisions are made that divide winners and losers, there can be no shared vision as a school and district. My-way-or-the-highway decision making may work in some situations, but must be avoided especially in those schools and school districts that strive to be as inclusive as possible. School administrators are confronted every day by conflicts over religious practices, evolution and creationist positions, sex education advocates and opponents, school board members pushing a political agenda, state and national accountability demands, segregation and school attendance boundaries, school spending, hiring practices, and conflicts between individuals at the campuses and central office personnel.

Scott Cutlip, Allen Center, and Glen Broom (1985, pp. 178–179) offer four research-based principles to ease conflict through effective persuasion. First is the *identification principle:* Most people will ignore an idea unless they see that it affects their personal fears, desires, hopes, or aspirations. Second is the *action principle:* People seldom buy ideas separated from action—either action taken by the sponsor of the idea or action taken by people to prove the merit of the idea. Third is the *familiarity and trust principle:* People buy ideas only from those they trust. Fourth is the *clarity principle:* The situation or idea must be easy to understand and clear, not subject to many interpretations. Leaders must use clear communication that includes symbols or models to persuade others.

If people perceive a school leader to be a person who possesses knowledge, communication skills, trust, and diplomacy, then that leader will be effective in influencing others about the need for policy changes to help students. Required readings in conflict resolution and skills in persuasion and diplomacy are mandatory for success in today's schools. Consequently, extensive training in conflict resolution should be part of every preparation program for school leaders. The following program could be created to meet this critical need.

- Identify successful conflict resolution models used in school districts and other agencies.
- Create a Conflict Resolution Task Force consisting of local teachers and selected religious and community leaders representing all ethnic groups, who can work with administrators and university professors to design the programs.
- Seek university, school district, and external funding to conduct the programs.
- Secure the services of a specialist in conflict resolution, and conduct training sessions for members of the Task Force.
- Create 1-hour graduate course work for all leadership education students and noncredit seminars for local school personnel selected for the training.

Business Training Works and other organizations suggest the following steps in creating successful conflict resolution seminars:

1. Identify factors that create conflict in the school and school district. Divide the task force into focus groups and use a modified *nominal group technique* to decide on the most frequent causes of conflict.

2. Appreciate how cultural and background diversity affect individual perceptions about situations. View videos and invite speakers to present valuable insights into diverse cultures, religions, and racial issues.

3. Emphasize the importance of listening skills to improve open (and sometimes emotional) communication. Invite an expert on communication, especially listening skills, to the task force meetings.

4. Evaluate the point of conflict—what is the real issue? Based on Step 1, the entire task force discusses each identified conflict factor and records the points of conflict on a flip chart for clarification.

5. Evaluate the conflict to determine if it can be solved or altered. Form three-member focus groups to make suggestions about solutions or other steps necessary to resolve the conflicts.

6. Understand the value of third-party facilitators when solutions are not easy to find. A conflict resolution consultant can

present reasons that third-party interventions can be valuable in reducing difficult conflicts between persons or groups.

7. Practice through role-playing simulations ways that the soul or spirit can guide individuals during conflict to avoid explosive confrontations.

8. Establish a procedure to handle conflicts in each school building and school district (including conflicts between board members and between board members and school personnel). The task force can then present a proposed process or policy to the school district and university professors for program planning.

The creation of a Conflict Resolution Task Force to design training for current and future school leaders is paramount in providing them with the skills to create change or perhaps become the moral compass and to bend the current rules to help students overcome circumstances beyond their control.

CONCLUSION

John Sanders is an example of the kind of person needed to lead America's schools. While he used his diplomacy and communication skills to alter the rules to help the Mexican American students, he also helped to create a collaborative learning community in his middle school.

Some have the soul for leadership in schools; others do not. If the soul for leadership is missing, any training in communication and diplomacy is wasted.

The soul of educational leadership is a complex mix of intellect, communication, values, and courage. Some have the soul for leadership in schools; others do not. If the soul for leadership is missing, any training in communication and diplomacy is wasted. Therefore, selecting candidates for graduate study reaches beyond communication skills and intellect or satisfactory GRE scores.

A thoughtful, deliberate plan to recruit individuals with records of selfless service and a compassion for building learning communities is the first criterion for selection. After selection, the aspiring leaders need extensive course work in diplomacy; communications; school operations and finance; policy; law; organizational theory/leadership; and multicultural, racial, ethnic, and religious issues, as well as real-world contact with and exposure to individuals and families mired in poverty.

In addition, aspiring school leaders need actual experience interacting with individuals excluded because of race or ethnic background. They need to spend time with agency leaders who serve the aged and infirm populations, with religious leaders serving the spiritual and other needs of individuals, and with city officials and law enforcement personnel who see the troubled side of society.

Finally, there is little doubt that serving as a school leader is more complicated and stressful with each passing decade. External pressures to improve high-stakes test scores, reduce violence and dropouts, hire greater numbers of minority and highly qualified teachers and administrators, and cope with family disturbances and greater numbers of students from single-parent homes call for conflict resolution skills and patience. Conflict resolution skills will not reduce all conflict, but by teaching future and current school administrators the necessary skills in communication and diplomacy, America's schools can become learning communities where all students succeed.

REFERENCES AND RELATED READINGS

Business Training Works. (2008). [Website] www.businesstrainingworks.com. Business Training Works, Inc., 9015 Katie Court, Port Tobacco, MD.

Chopra, D. (2002). The soul of leadership. *The school administrator,* 8(59), 10–14.

Cutlip, S. M., Center, A. H., & Broom, G. M. (1985). *Effective public relations* (6th ed.). Englewood Cliffs, NJ: Prentice Hall.

Griffiths, D. (1964). The nature and meaning of theory. In D. Griffiths (Ed.), *Behavioral science and educational administration* (Yearbook of the National Society for the Study of Education [new ser.] 63d, pt. 2, pp. 95–118). Chicago: University of Chicago Press.

Houston, P. D., & Sokolow, S. L. (2006). *The spiritual dimension of leadership.* Thousand Oaks, CA: Corwin.

Hoy, W. K., & Miskel, C. G. (2007). *Educational administration: Theory and practice.* Boston: McGraw-Hill.

Hoyle, J. (2002). *Leadership and the force of love.* Thousand Oaks, CA: Corwin.

Hoyle, J. (2007). *Leadership and futuring: Making visions happen.* Thousand Oaks, CA: Corwin.

Hoyle, J., Bjork, L., Collier, V., & Glass, T. (2005). *The superintendent as CEO: Standards-based performance.* Thousand Oaks, CA: Corwin.

Hoyle, J., & Crenshaw, H. (1997). *Interpersonal sensitivity.* Larchmont, NY: Eye on Education.

Hoyle, J., English, F., & Steffy, B. (1998). *Skills for successful 21st century school leaders.* Lanham, MD: R & L Education/Rowman & Littlefield.

Moore, T. (1992). *Care of the soul.* New York: Harper Perennial.

Nichols, S. L., & Berliner, D. C. (2007). *Collateral damage.* Cambridge, MA: Harvard Education Press.

Owens, R. G., & Valesky, T. (2007). *Organizational behavior in education.* Boston: Pearson Press.

Thomas, K. (1976). Conflict and conflict management. In M. D. Dunnette (Ed.), *Handbook of industrial and organizational psychology.* Chicago: Rand McNally.

CHAPTER FOUR

LEARNING TO BE
A LEADER

BETTY ROSA

I arrived in District 8—in the Bronx, New York—on March 15, 1998. My journey to the superintendent's job in District 8 had been quite a ride, and in a way it was a homecoming for me. Though I was born in New York City, I spent the first 10 years of my life in Puerto Rico, then moved back to New York in the early 1960s. Back then, there was no bilingual education, no "transitional" programs. Though my English skills were limited, I was literate in Spanish.

I attended public schools in the Bronx, in Districts 9 and 10, and later attended St. Helena's High School. I graduated from high school in 3½ years, then enrolled in City College of New York and pursued a major in psychology, finishing my bachelor's degree in 3 years. I carried with me the knowledge that others like me could achieve an education—and might, also like me, lead others to do so.

I began teaching in the New York City schools in 1974, having also worked as a paraprofessional, or teaching assistant, during college. Still in the Bronx, I taught Grades 2 through 6 in District 9. During this time, I completed a master's degree in bilingual education; about 8 years later I began earning another master's degree (also at City College) toward a certification in administration and supervision, and I completed an internship at the New York City Board of Education headquarters in the Division of Special Education. In completing this course of training, I was now, according to the State of New York, "qualified" to serve in administrative and supervisory capacities at all levels in a school system.

In 1991, however, I came to a turning point in my development as a leader. That summer I attended the Principals Leadership Program at Harvard University. I realized then that I had been on an educational fast track without spending the time to understand the deeper meaning of what I was studying and the best practices available to achieve results. I realized, too, that learning is an ongoing process. I would forever look at my role as an educational leader in a different light from that point, having discovered that learning to be a leader cannot take place solely in a lecture hall or a graduate school classroom.

I realized that learning is an ongoing process. I would forever look at my role as an educational leader in a different light, having discovered that learning to be a leader cannot take place solely in a lecture hall or a graduate school classroom.

While at Harvard, my outspokenness apparently brought me to the attention of the faculty; my "New York spirit" garnered me an invitation to enroll in the Urban Superintendent's Program (USP) at the Harvard Graduate School of Education in 1992. The USP essentially had two goals for students: (1) to get students familiar with the theoretical concepts of educational leadership, focusing on research and culminating in a dissertation; and (2) to have them complete a full-time internship in an urban school district to observe and learn in a real-life setting. The aim was to prepare students for the practical side of the superintendent's role.

The USP introduced me to the value of mentoring. Paul Houston, then a member of the USP superintendents' network and a future American Association of School Administrators (AASA) president (and executive director), helped to guide me through the doctoral process as well as my transition into a superintendency. This was the first time that a practicing superintendent had offered me advice and direction grounded in real-world experience. The Harvard program would continue to expose us to other mentors and provide opportunities to observe varying styles of leadership.

The USP program included both university-based authorities talking about issues of leadership and sitting superintendents discussing their world and the everyday issues that they were confronting. Although most of the superintendents with whom I interacted were male, the concepts and the knowledge they shared had universal themes. Hearing the issues and daunting challenges facing urban superintendents (the focus of our program), I sometimes had second thoughts about becoming a superintendent. The political aspect of the job seemed very challenging to me and a waste of good energy, and it was unrelated to any of my prior experience, training, and course work. Nonetheless, I was still not ready to rule out the possibility.

Upon completing the USP course work, I began the next leg of my journey: the internship, which required me to shadow a superintendent. I landed in New York City's District 10 with John Reehill, who allowed me to focus primarily on the relationship between the board and superintendent, an area I had always been uneasy about. During those 6 months, I saw everything that could go wrong when the romance between the superintendent and the board is over. The district felt like a place where people were divided, like a marriage going through a bitter divorce: reconciliation was simply not possible. I saw quickly that an atmosphere lacking trust and respect cannot produce positive results for children. I observed board meetings with constant disagreements, bickering, and outright fighting. Every meeting began with accusations and statements of the dysfunctional nature of the superintendent and his administration. Several board members regularly made public requests that the superintendent "step down."

During this horrific experience, I came to feel that every negative lesson one could learn about the relationship between the superintendent and board existed in this district. I internalized all the "what-not-to-do" lessons I experienced firsthand, and those lessons stay with me to this day.

During the summer of 1994, having completed my dissertation, I returned to my previous position as principal of a special education school. In October 1995, I took a position as principal of a large intermediate school (approximately 2,000 students) in the Washington Heights section of Manhattan, a largely Dominican community. The school embraced a "full-service" approach to serving children and the community and made use of resources from the district, the Carnegie Foundation, the Children's Aid Society, and a variety of community organizations. Often referred to by the superintendent as the district's "flagship" school, it was the archetype of what is possible in an otherwise underserved environment. The school had a dental clinic, family services, a full-time psychiatrist, a psychologist, counselors, several assistant principals, and theme-based academies. We had partnerships with the Alvin Ailey Dance Company, Ballet Hispanico, and Morgan Stanley in providing internships for our students. We had a store in the school, a radio station, and an architecture studio. Our doors were open to the community from 7 AM to 10 PM, 6 days a week. Compared to my internship, where I learned how *not* to do things in an urban school, this experience clearly demonstrated the incredible possibilities when everyone keeps in mind that our mission is to truly care for and educate children.

Then, in late 1996, I received a call from Rudy Crew, chancellor of the New York City public schools, to assume the leadership role of a struggling school district. I had first met Chancellor Crew at the USP program at Harvard, where he served as a mentor. Though flattered by his offer, I was truly enjoying my intermediate school and felt that it was too soon for me to move on. I also felt that my internship experience in District 10 had not fully prepared me to deal with an urban superintendency. After some discussions with Chancellor Crew, however (and after the state legislature gave him the authority to select new superintendents), I applied for the superintendency of a troubled district in the Bronx, but was not chosen by the board.

At the same time, a neighboring district, District 8, was selecting a new superintendent, and this time I was hired for the job. Once selected, with 2 months to prepare for my new role, I began by putting together a small transition team to analyze the various aspects of the district, from the budget to student performance. Several issues emerged as clear priorities. One prominent problem was the racial division that had existed for many years and that was reflected by the composition of the school board and its voting on many issues. The second issue was that most parents sent their

My aim was to begin to articulate the district's needs, start to educate my board members about these needs, set the initial direction for the district, and elicit the board's support in moving the district ahead.

children to the local elementary schools, but not to our middle schools. Clearly one challenge was to strengthen the middle schools.

My transition team also analyzed student achievement and the performance of each district school. Although most of the schools were *not* performing well, the district's internal perception was that they were doing better than was actually the case. We rated schools according to student performance and examined the distribution of resources across schools. We began to create a preliminary plan for dealing with all of these issues. My aim was to begin to articulate the district's needs, start to educate my board members about these needs, set the initial direction for the district, and elicit the board's support in moving the district ahead.

My first actions were centered on building a sense of unity within District 8, which had been divided along racial and economic lines. Some groups in the community felt that they had been marginalized by the previous superintendent and board. The board had been involved in many public fights. As one example, several lawsuits were pending in which board members were suing one another, and there was a lawsuit filed by the board's secretary against a board member. Issues of power, control, and influence seemed to consume the board; discussions about curriculum, programs, and resources for children and teachers were not priorities at board meetings. It was a mess, to say the least, and the district's children were paying the price. I needed to begin to create opportunities for the board members to come together. And, while we were creating a sense of unity, my second challenge was to rally the community to support our schools. I wanted more parental involvement. I started meeting with elected officials throughout the district, as well as neighborhood organizations and other groups that could support various aspects of the job that needed to get done. I articulated my vision and enlisted everyone's assistance.

When I officially reported for work, in March 1998, I began to interview staff, reassuring them that they should continue their work until we could develop a shared vision for the district. I wanted staff members to get through the transition without creating chaos in the schools. To me, the culture within the district seemed rather self-serving; it felt as if the district's primary function—to educate children—was not even being stated, let alone reinforced. The principals felt that the district operated in a "punitive" manner and that they received little support. Therefore I initiated a campaign to support the schools, starting with informing the district staff that they were there *for* the schools and needed to become advocates for their schools. At the same time, I started work every morning by visiting schools. I wanted to clearly demonstrate by example that the children and the schools were the priority.

By May 1998, I had begun to address each segment of the racially divided district as well as the problem of losing middle school students to private schools. I decided that I needed to make a statement and create a direction on each of these two fronts. As one example, I had a school building occupied primarily by New York City Board of Education employees in the Throgs Neck area of the district. I told those staff members that I was moving them to a different location, since I saw no reason for having a school building occupied primarily by adults. The building would be a terrific place to start a special program for middle school students.

As I shared my concept for a new school with the board and the community, I explained that we would start small and grow into a middle school of no more than 600 students. The rest of the space would be used for a new lab school for K–4 students. I wanted to create a lab school centered on best practices where teachers would have professional development opportunities.

We created an outreach campaign to draw in the first 100 students for the new school. We explained that we were creating a middle school of choice for those District 8 children who scored at levels 3 or 4 on the state test. In addition to high scores on the test, we planned to take into account teacher recommendations and grades. In order to assure a diverse student body, however, we decided that we would have to guarantee that students from every elementary school in the district would be represented, by means of a random intraschool lottery selection and then through an at-large lottery among qualified students.

Amazingly, the new school—the first step in the unification and healing process for the district—was up and running by the following September. At the same time, I was making a statement about what we needed our middle schools to look like. I promised the community that Maritime/101, as we named the school, was established as a partnership with the Maritime College in the Throgs Neck area, and that it would be the first of several new magnet schools in the district. We selected Teach for America as a source for teachers and developed an innovative type of personalized program. The school became extremely popular throughout the district, and parents began talking about getting their children into the school. Maritime/101 had a diverse student body by design, which became its strength. We had children who lived in protective shelters, as well as the children of lawyers and judges. The level of excitement about the school gave the district a sense of excitement and hope for the future. I wanted parents throughout the district to feel that they were being consulted

I wanted parents throughout the district to feel that they were being consulted and that they had real choices about their children's education.

and that they had real choices about their children's education. This feeling would later be strengthened in the district through "choice" fairs that allowed parents and students to get a feeling for what various schools offered.

Unfortunately, the school board, while excited about the new middle school, continued with some of their old ways. The manner in which the board was functioning was characterized by persistent friction and fighting. Though individually they were willing to work with me, when they had to work with each other tempers flared again and again. I realized quickly that I needed to focus on my board and how their working together to support the children of District 8 was critical to the ultimate success of the district. I needed to develop a strategy to help the board members learn how to act as a responsible group of adults and focus their energies on their responsibilities and commitment to the children.

My efforts were aimed at creating a sense of "common unity" leading to a real sense of community, and creating opportunities to celebrate the things that bonded us as a district. We needed to accept with humility the "gifts" that we give each other every day. One question I asked the board to use as a filter for discussions was, "What does this issue have to do with student achievement?" I told the board members that I didn't want to be the superintendent of adults. That was part of my work, but I wanted to be seen as the *superintendent of children.* Our students didn't have the protection of the unions. They had me—the 800-pound gorilla—to protect them. So, for the students, it was vitally important for me to have the capacity and the authority to transform others and to build relationships through our dialogues. We had to have a purpose and a passion to support the children of District 8.

The second year, we introduced magnets within every middle school. Our schools were moving in the right direction, and the community was feeling that they had a voice in their children's education. Attendance at board meetings increased, the meetings were conducted professionally, district successes were celebrated, and student performances and award ceremonies were conducted at many of the meetings. I surrounded myself with a strong team of hardworking individuals who were willing to put in 10- to 15-hour days. I could see that staff members were giving the district their heart and soul. As a leader, I had found ways to model and to motivate our staff to support our shared vision.

By 1999, we had a district that would work hard but also knew how to celebrate its accomplishments. We had great attendance at the new parent-organized dinners, which were an opportunity to share a sense of family and a feeling that "we're all in this together." I loved going to work. I felt a rush of energy every day. Like a kid at a carnival, I loved every ride. I felt that while we were focused on instruction and adding rigor to our delivery system and curriculum, we were also connecting at all levels. The most important lesson for me was the importance of everyone understanding our interdependence.

Over the next 2 years, we saw an improvement in test results, better working conditions for our principals, and more resources. The district office was downsized to give more money to the schools, where all agreed that the needs were more acute. Here was truly a statement about what really mattered. We continued to meet in small and large groups to discuss our direction and to make sure that we were doing what we said we were going to do. We had retreats and shared our personal stories as a way of solidifying our bonding process. I felt that I was facilitating the empowerment of the staff and our partners in District 8.

If all of this feels as if it was too good to last, it was. In December 1999, conflicts between Mayor Rudolph Giuliani and Chancellor Crew resulted in the chancellor's departure—and in the city losing one of our most charismatic educational leaders. Rudy Crew provided his district superintendents with "food to feed their soul." He inspired us to be more than we could ever have imagined. His departure was a terrible blow to all who were connected to his mission of finding strategies to support urban students.

Shortly thereafter, I was asked by the new chancellor, Harold Levy, to assume the post of "senior superintendent" for the borough of the Bronx, even though I was not at all convinced that a superintendent in charge of each of the five boroughs was the best model for running the enormous New York City system. I agreed to accept the assignment as long as I could keep the superintendency of District 8. It was a tough time for me, since I was both continuing my work as superintendent and supporting the other districts in the Bronx. I had doubts about my ability to do this type of mentoring, since I myself was still developing as a superintendent. Nonetheless, I was determined to do my best.

I held the dual positions—superintendent of District 8 and, at the same time, the senior superintendency—for about 2 years. In June 2002, another mayor, Michael Bloomberg, appointed yet another new chancellor. This was a turning point in my career as a superintendent, as I watched the organization that I had grown up with begin to restructure, yet again—from the days of demands for community control to essentially the total elimination of any relevant community involvement.

This was a turning point in my career as a superintendent, as I watched the organization that I had grown up with begin to restructure, yet again—from the days of demands for community control to essentially the total elimination of any relevant community involvement.

The deputy chancellor, Diana Lam, told us how our local boards were to be eliminated; I knew in my heart that we were next. I did not feel connected with the new leadership, nor did I trust them. I felt that we were about to embark on a style of leadership that was not aligned with my own sense of leadership. At a well-staged public meeting on January 15, 2003, all of us superintendents were charged with having used and abused the poor minority children. I was furious. I refused to allow the mayor to rewrite my history. I had come to the Bronx as a child, and I grew up in the Bronx promising to one day "give back." I knew that the mayor was out of touch with the realities of the system and was misguided in believing that the new chancellor—who had no experience in leading a school, let alone the largest school district in the country—knew what was best for children. I remember one superintendent telling me that we all have issues or hills that we will die on in this job. I prepared myself for my own particular hill.

That January 15 meeting marked the end for me. I shared with my principals, my board members, and the community my decision to leave the system. Though there were several demonstrations against the chancellor in an attempt to keep me as the superintendent of District 8, I explained to the parents, staff, community, and board that I had no desire to remain in this new organization. It was simply not a good fit for me.

On June 30, 2003, I resigned from the New York City Department of Education and left behind a special part of my life. I mourned the loss of the district as if I had lost a loved one—which, in fact, I had. I have continued my work in education, but it will be most difficult for me to regain the same sense of passion and purpose that I felt for District 8. I felt that I had unified a racially divided community for the common good of all of its children. I stayed true to the mission, created a clear and shared vision, and led by setting the right example to be emulated by all. I had acted as if all of the children were my own. I danced to my own rhythm while those associated with the mayor's office danced with two left feet. My youngest son graduated from a District 8 middle school during my tenure. His experiences in one of the most culturally diverse schools in the city will last a lifetime, as will mine.

Early in my career, I realized that leadership is a personal journey that allows us to connect our inner world with the world that we want to affect. I have come to picture myself as leaving my footprints for all those who will follow and extend and deepen whatever I have been able to do. It is through our interaction and interdependence that we create meaning. In District 8, the Bronx, I helped create a lifetime of meaning, both for myself and for all those whose lives I was fortunate enough to touch.

CHAPTER FIVE

LEADERS AS COMMUNICATORS AND AMBASSADORS

RICH BAGIN

Looking back on favorite teachers who helped to shape my personal and professional attributes, I remember the words of one management consultant who focused on a set of principles that have driven my brand of leadership for more than 20 years. Ken Schatz, author of *Managing by Influence* (1986), taught many kernels of wisdom, but two continue to influence me today:

- You can never *not* lead.
- Ask yourself, what did I do (or not do) to make this happen (or not happen)?

Superintendents, central office leaders, principals, and other leaders can become more effective communicators and ambassadors by applying his advice to their style of leadership.

You Can Never Not Lead

Create a Culture of Communication

As a school leader, you are always "on" in today's 24/7 world. Whether you're talking to parents at a ball game, greeting business leaders at the supermarket, visiting with staff in one of your schools, or catching a community theater production, you *will* be noticed and you *will* leave an impression. Your visibility and status within your schools and your community will be measured as an indicator of your caring and commitment about your schools and community.

—————— ✂ ——————

As a school leader, you are always "on" in today's 24/7 world. Your visibility and status within your schools and your community will be measured as an indicator of your caring and commitment about your schools and community.

You can never *not* lead when it comes to establishing a culture of communication in your schools and community. Our experiences at the National School Public Relations Association (NSPRA) show us that the most successful school communication programs start at the top, with leaders who are committed to the importance of communication and who then make sure that all central office leaders, principals, and other supervisors follow through on that commitment. This commitment translates into action. When a major decision is called for, successful leaders ask how the decision will be communicated, make sure that it is communicated, and then confirm that the loop is closed on all engagement and communication efforts. These leaders hold themselves and their staff members accountable for their communication efforts by making communication a criterion in annual evaluations.

Lead the Way in Choosing the Substance of Your Communication Effort

Leadership in the type of communication programs or activities you offer is another factor of the guiding principle that "You can never *not* lead." Successful superintendents are the gatekeepers when it comes to communication. Decisions on how big or small the effort should be, what it should accomplish, and who actually implements elements of the program rest with the superintendent.

Some superintendents are hell-bent on developing a make-us-look-good program whose major objective is to build the images of the leaders and the district. Others focus on how communication fits into the long-range plan and yearly goals and objectives of their systems. And some have begun developing programs that center on student achievement, home–school communication with parents, two-way internal and operational communication, and building a climate of support for instructional initiatives in their communities.

Leading superintendents know that fitting the communication effort into their goals and objectives and focusing on student achievement are the best ways to build a positive reputation for their districts. That is where you must make the commitment. Your ongoing communication efforts will have more staying power—and you will extend the tenure of your superintendency.

Some superintendents object that their personality does not lend itself to being a great communicator. Certainly not everyone has the charm and wit of Ronald Reagan. Nonetheless, every superintendent who wants to succeed must commit to creating the elements of a comprehensive communication program.

Superintendents' commitment may be measured by whether they do the right things: research, planning, implementing relationship-building tactics, and evaluating them. If you have a smaller district, you can teach and empower current staff to become better communicators for your schools. If you're in a larger system, you should have professional communication assistance; it will make a huge difference if you spend time on all the right things.

The superintendent's commitment sets the communication culture for the district. When you make communication a priority, you'll begin building a foundation of positive relationships with your staff, parents, and community leaders.

Create Trust and Integrity
Through Authentic Communication

Relationships are at the heart of any program of communication and ambassadorship, and relationships are built on trust and integrity. Once you lose the trust of your board, community leaders, staff, and parents, it's time to call, "Check, please!" and get out of Dodge as soon as you can.

Two illustrations from communication audits I completed in the past few years make this point. The first dealt with a president of a Canadian community college who described his personal leadership strength as listening to his staff and practicing collaborative communication while working with them. His staff thought differently. One instructor noted that the president did practice "management by walking around," and gave the impression that he was in touch with his faculty. This instructor noted that the president had stopped by his room just before class and asked him how he was doing. The instructor told the president that he had just placed his mother, who had terminal cancer, in a nursing home and that she had only a month or so to live. The president's quick response was, "Glad to hear it. Keep up the good work." True story. Others confirmed it and reinforced the idea that the president's self-anointed strength was a sham. He did not listen to his staff, nor did he involve them in any decision making, let alone in authentic small talk. No matter what that president did, he could never regain credibility and trust with the faculty in that institution.

The second illustration is of a superintendent who also proved less than authentic with his staff members. Again, during a communication audit, we were reviewing the superintendent's practice of sending cards to staff on their birthdays. The system was fairly large—more than 1,500 employees. Sending cards became a duty of a staff member who worked in the immediate area of the superintendent's office.

The system was in the midst of teacher negotiations. Many cards were sent back to the superintendent with notes indicating that he should stop this process. However, he persisted. Then a card came back from the staff member whose job it was to complete all of the cards that were sent out. This card contained a note saying, "I am the person who sends the cards for you. You walk by my desk at least four times a day. All you needed to do was wish me a Happy Birthday. Instead, I received the card that *I* prepared for you. I bet you don't even know my name." Unbelievably, the superintendent continued to send the cards, thus adding to his staff's animosity.

> *Losing credibility and trust with your staff is one of the quickest ways to sink your communication and leadership efforts. . . . In our work, we see the lack of follow-up as one of the trust-busters that impede authentic communication.*

Neither of these leaders is still in his respective position. Both thought that through their symbolic actions, they were communicating. The sad reality is that they *were* communicating, but people perceived their communication, accurately, as phony and insensitive.

Leading productivity consultants such as Tom Peters and others tell us to be effective and sensitive communicators with all our staff because they are the ones who carry the ball for us, work it down the field, and score the touchdowns for our organizations. Losing credibility and trust with your staff is one of the quickest ways to sink your communication and leadership efforts.

Our work with school districts around the country also tells us that to build an authentic communication program we need to listen to people carefully and then communicate what we did or did not do based on their input. In our work, we see the lack of follow-up as one of the trust-busters that impede authentic communication. More often than not, during communication audits parents tell us that their districts ask them to provide input on some upcoming issues. The parents follow through and give their input—and that's the last they hear from anyone. The result is that those parents feel "used"; they end up believing that school leaders already know what they want to do and use community input only to confirm their thoughts. They feel that their time has been wasted and that the entire "engagement" activity is a sham. Rather than building partnerships and credibility, such non-authentic practices serve as trust-busters for any future calls for input from staff, parents, and community leaders.

Transparency and Public Engagement: Don't Start a Communication Program Without Them

Transparency and the vital importance of public engagement with your schools follow from the previous discussion of the importance of authenticity. The only way to build trust and integrity in your leadership is to practice transparency in all school operations—warts and all. A leaking roof, gaps in achievement, misbehaving staff—all need to be explained with a statement of what you are doing about whatever the issue is.

Even more important, however, is the authentic engagement of community and staff to partner with you in moving forward on key issues. Building public engagement is hard and sometimes discouraging work. It's like going on a diet: you start slowly, but after some work and sacrifice, you begin seeing results. Public engagement follows the same course. It's often difficult to corral the interested residents to help you start from "zero" on issues. Furthermore, it's also difficult for your board and other administrators to start from the same "zero-based" approach. Don't go in with your own solutions and try to persuade residents of the school district to follow them. That's not public engagement.

Authentic engagement is wide open and transparent and eventually leads to a greatly improved understanding of the school district's capabilities and needs. And it begins building a culture of integrity and credibility in your leadership.

WHAT DID I DO (OR NOT DO) TO MAKE THIS HAPPEN (OR NOT HAPPEN)?

The second bit of advice from Ken Schatz will ring true for you as you look back at your career as a school leader. We have all had times when we found ourselves in a controversy or dilemma that we know could have been avoided if we had taken some previous action. It's always best to remember that you can't unscramble scrambled eggs.

A large part of being a leader of a successful school system or school building is to anticipate issues or situations, run "what-if scenarios," and then make the best decisions to move forward and earn the respect and protect the reputation of your system—and yourself as well.

Examples of sticky situations include the following:

- Allowing a less-than-effective teacher who has a blemished record to continue teaching at one of your very competitive high schools.
- Making school boundary changes that make little logical sense to parents and not communicating about them or creating any opportunities for understanding.
- Expecting a "renegade" board member not to be seen as *the* spokesperson for the board.

Leading superintendents make the time to anticipate situations. And leading superintendents also do more to make it known what they and their systems stand for.

- Not having all your athletic coaches verify the academic and geographical eligibility rules for their students.
- Not taking accountability measures regarding student activity funds and the use of related credit cards for those funds.

In the past 2 years, these situations were the subject of just some of the counseling calls NSPRA provided to superintendents and their staff. All of these situations could have been avoided if someone had taken preventive action. And when this type of muck hits the fan, guess who's charged with the major blame for allowing these actions to occur? So we're back to Ken Schatz's question: "What did you do or not do to make this happen?"

Leading superintendents make the time to anticipate such situations. And leading superintendents also do more to make it known what they and their systems stand for.

Taking Action: Credo
Cards Make a Difference

One such forward-thinking superintendent is Dr. Rodney Lafon of the St. Charles Parish Public Schools in Luling, Louisiana. At NSPRA, we often ask school employees if they know where their school district is headed, or what major initiatives are underway, or what their district stands for. Most times we hear negative replies: "No" or "Not really; it doesn't matter anyway."

Unlike some leaders, Rodney Lafon wanted to counter this common response before it had time to form in his schools. He created a *Credo Card* for the St. Charles Parish Public Schools. During an interview with NSPRA, here's what Dr. Lafon said about creating his Credo Cards:

Well, you know, I took an idea from the Ritz Carlton and it's called a Credo Card. The Credo Card that we developed has a mission, vision, and beliefs on it and then it has our credo, which is simply: *Core business teaching and learning, our commitment of learning for life and our focus on continuous improvement.*

And as we developed the card, we also developed the branding, which is *You and I . . . We Are St. Charles Parish Public Schools.* That is on the Credo Card as you open it up.

THE MISSION

of St. Charles Parish Public Schools is to provide

high quality educational opportunities

to enable its students to become

responsible, productive citizens and **enthusiastic life-long learners.**

The citizens of St. Charles Parish place the education of their children as a top priority.

Education is a shared responsibility of the schools, students, families, St. Charles Parish Public School System staff, school board, local government agencies, higher education and the business community. There is a commitment from stakeholders to help all students to become life-long learners. Our schools foster a love of learning, and our schools equip students with the knowledge and skills required to lead productive and fulfilling lives in the changing society of the 21st century.

- **Education** is society's first priority.
- **All** students can learn.
- **Supportive** work environments enable students and staff to demonstrate mutual respect and reach their potential for life-long learning.
- **Students and staff** meet high-expectations for achievement and success by engaging in challenging and relevant work.
- **Open and honest** communication builds trust.
- **Excellence** is worth the cost.

Source: Reprinted with permission from St. Charles Parish Public Schools.

We took the Credo Cards and visited every employee in St. Charles Parish School System. I talked to them about the Credo Card and how I got the idea from the Ritz Carlton and how everyone in the Ritz Carlton carries their card and can actually recite the mission of the Ritz Carlton. Their credo is very simple: *Ladies and Gentlemen Serving Ladies and Gentlemen.*

Now if you think about the powerful messages you send, most people in the organization will be able to understand that our core business is teaching and learning. When you conduct staff focus groups or meetings, you introduce the participants to the card. I don't require that people carry the card in the organization, but I'll tell you this: I'll ask that they carry the card with pride.

So as you walk in[to] St. Charles Parish Public Schools, everybody is aware of the Credo Card, though they may not be able to recite the card exactly. Because of that simple credo of *core business teaching and learning, our commitment of learning for life and our focus on continuous improvement,* they understand what we are all about. It has been very powerful and has taken our organization a long way.

You can walk down the hall of our local hospital these days, and somebody will point at you and say, *You and I . . . We Are St. Charles Parish Public Schools.* So it is a way of getting your message out and a way for us to bring pride to the organization. And every year when new employees come in, I meet with all of them and go through the Credo Card and we talk about what we are about. It has worked marvelously for us.

Rodney Lafon took a situation in which staff was vague about the core mission of their school district and did something about it. He didn't just have cards printed and distributed; he also speaks at every school and meets with new employees each year to convey the importance of their mission. Lafon's practice has built teamwork and a sense of pride and enthusiasm among his staff and community.

Taking Action: Making Noise to Engage the Traditionally Unengaged

A second positive example of taking or not taking action comes from Superintendent Rudy Crew in the Miami-Dade County

Schools in Florida. Recently, I was part of an American Association of School Administrators (AASA) panel with Rudy and other superintendents and communication specialists. The discussion led to how superintendents are portrayed through the media. Controversy on budgets, board versus administration priorities, or the latest crisis incident in one of the schools are what normally fill the pages and airwaves about today's urban superintendents. As Rudy said during this panel, most of the work superintendents do seems defined by what the media portrays. But he is determined to change that portrayal:

> Part of our work in Miami is to flip that and say the work is about *children.* Any and everything we do and any and everything we commit to has to be seen in the context of powerful people doing powerful work. And that became the way by which, theoretically at least, we began to think about how do we get that message out there and what are the tools necessary for being able to do that. How would we brand that message? How would you create energy in a campaign around that message? It's fundamentally not about the mayor's relationship with me or the superintendent's relationship with the board. Or whatever the crisis du jour is—it is not about that. There has to be a trump card. And unless the district has a strategic methodology on how to create this trump card, you are almost always sub-optimized because you are always subject to the whim, the description, the context of the press. And that becomes your only way of being able to be known by your marketplace, by your consumers.
>
> So the sense that I have is that first of all, we've got to flip the coin here from the total supply side to the demand side. In Miami, we no longer wanted to have a conversation with parents or the business community or anyone else based on the assumption of what you need to do for us, or what you need to give to us, or can you come to a meeting about us.
>
> It needs to be more about your demanding what doesn't exist in this system. You are consumers of this system. You make use of the assets of this system in a way that makes you more of a demand if you use it than supply. And what we found is that in the poorer communities in our district—places with a large immigrant population, large populations whose first language is

not English—we had very high mountains to climb on the demand side because parents didn't demand *anything.* They were totally supply-side parents. Bring their babies to school and whatever you tell me to do, I will if I can. My relationship with those parents as a district was a relationship predicated upon their just simply doing the minimum: "Just bring the baby in." And for them the relationship with us was: "At least do no harm." "Just do the best you can." We said, "No. We can't have that kind of relationship with you. That can't be the way this goes because you need to actually be an asset in your child's life if we're going to win. This kid's going to graduate on time with the skills, and you need to be in this play."

During the panel discussion, Crew reviewed how he and his staff developed a marketing campaign to help change the mind-set of parents and community leaders so that they could be successful in their schools. His messages and tactics were bold—and even crossed the line of being controversial for most of today's superintendents. He wanted to stir controversy, so he helped to create it. That took courage. He readily admits that his system, with more than 350,000 students, is still working on this strategy of "flipping" the traditional messages, but they're making progress.

And by the way, because of this work in the Miami-Dade County Schools, Crew was named the 2008 National Superintendent of the Year at the annual AASA convention.

Crew talks about his "noisemaking" in this way:

Our objective was a very strategic communications plan as part of our overall plan. Our objective was to flip the switch from supply-side thinking from poor parents to demand side. So the noisier it got, the better. The more raucous parents were about "How come you are making our kids go to school later or earlier?" "How come you added an 8th-period day?"—I wanted to have that conversation. So much so that in a couple of cases, I threatened to close a bunch of schools in these communities and, in the course of doing that, I had to go out to community town halls in those high

The media isn't the driver of your message; you become the driver of that message and, hence, the superintendency.

school gyms and say to them, "Here's why I'm going to close your school."

I had lists of bad performance year after year—problems in their athletic program, problems in the staffing in schools, whatever it may have been. And what I got back was, "How dare you!" And that is exactly what I wanted this moment to be. I didn't enjoy it, but it's exactly what you want.

You *want* this engaged relationship, even if it is around tension. But you want this engaged relationship in which you can say back, "I dare do this because you aren't engaged." So the relationship now flips. Now from, "Oh, you are doing this to me" to a relationship of "No, then we need to do something with and for each other." So it becomes a quid pro quo.

But it really was a kind of a strategy of simply saying this isn't about *this* issue. This is about your being on the demand side and not sitting back and expecting the school system to carry your child through four years of high school, then hunt you down every time they're absent and make you try to come in and help with the child's homework. And make you participate in this child's life. I'm saying that you love this child; you brought this child onto this earth. Then, by God, here is *your* responsibility. And mine to you is to give you the tools to be able to do that.

So the theory was to flip the switch from supply-side thinking in our community to demand-side thinking. We're not completely there, but the theory is alive and well in Miami.

I understand that it is perilous, and it gives the newspaper secondary space in your life as opposed to primary space. The media isn't the driver of your message; *you* become the driver of that message and, hence, the superintendency. Your time is optimized in the communication of that message as opposed to being sub-optimized. You are no longer the end of the story; you are the beginning of the story.

Taking Action: Attacking Core Assumptions

Crew also used his communication effort to attack many long-held myths about urban students. Instead of simply doing the usual things in communication, he created new messages and then made sure—as best he could—that these messages were received and understood by key populations in his enormous community.

Here's what he had to say about his message process:

We needed to be at the core assumptions level. So we blew away a lot of the old assumptions in preference for some new ones. Here are some old assumptions that had to be taken on, and are still in the process of being taken on:

1. Poor parents won't or can't participate.
2. Parents in urban communities don't have the skill to help do this work.
3. There is not enough money to be able to affect the change that we need.
4. Children, particularly those whose first language is not English, children who are poor, children of any color, children who are afflicted by a whole set of urban issues, are somehow always going to be at the end of the line in being able to reach statewide or global standards.

We are going to aim our communication plans [at] core assumptions. Core assumptions of teachers, parents, business community—all that stuff had to be blown away. These people believe that they can't do it. And what we ended up having to say is that we need a system and a plan that aims at core assumptions of an organization.

At the end of the day, you want core assumptions to be challenged and changed. And we needed to harness this to a full-scope campaign. This wasn't going to be just a newsletter here and there, a couple of phone calls, meetings—in separate, isolated ways. These all had to be aligned so that they actually worked in unison. So I had, for example, on a monthly basis, a meeting with 25 business leaders through the entire city, being able to reach out to those people with the building of a relationship and helping them to flip the switch from supply to demand.

Most don't know what is going on in the school district, and some say why don't you have a better communication plan or marketing. And that became part and parcel of an entire array, a whole strategy around communication.

[It was important that] the campaign . . . have one, clear, and predominant voice. It has to drown out all other craziness in the district. Every time a board member yells at me and calls me crazy, the press goes wild. Have something louder and ready for that. So you can literally send a message about things that are really important that always trumped the minutiae of the day.

Second, you must have focused and meaningful [subject] matter. Clear and focused attention on things that matter. I send messages about children's statewide tests, saying that I would care about your child no matter how he did. A much bigger and more powerful message. [Crew uses the Connect-Ed messaging service, which is the market leader in this field.]

Last but not least, they want to have an ongoing relationship with you. By using our messaging connection system, I receive positive feedback about being personal with the community. They want to have a connection with you.

Crew and his staff are still slugging it out to change the perception of urban students and get more parents and community leaders engaged in their school community. He truly fits the category of "never not leading" and taking action when needed.

Taking Action: Holding a
Community Connection Mixer

Dr. Ken Bird, veteran superintendent of the Westside Community Schools in Omaha, Nebraska, has been participating in early morning weekday breakfast sessions with the movers and shakers of his Greater Omaha community for many years. Every morning, Bird makes his way to the local breakfast spot, The Market Basket, with no real agenda in mind, and meets with local business leaders, government officials, and other community and parent leaders before his day at work officially begins. Topics cover the entire scope of whatever is on the minds of these leaders. On some days, they don't even discuss school issues.

State legislators, and even the governor, have been known to drop in, along with the mayor and other city leaders. One observer of this daily confab says, "It's like a bunch of married couples reading their papers over breakfast. First they read, then they chat or leave to go to work."

Bird knows that this time he spends virtually every morning when he's in town is one of the best ways of staying in touch with the leadership network in his community. All of them know that he is accessible, and he too can tap leaders who can influence major issues for his school district community for input. Bird makes the commitment to this type of ambassadorship because he knows it is time well spent.

Taking Action: Research
Before You Communicate

The old E. F. Hutton commercial in which everyone tries to listen to some sage investment advice is the setup for the next action step. If you want to know the secret of communication success for school systems, it is *research*.

Research gives you the knowledge necessary to build an efficient and effective program. Through research, you'll learn what your critical publics know and what they don't know. You'll learn the best, preferred ways of reaching them and affecting their opinion on upcoming issues.

Research gives you the knowledge necessary to build an efficient and effective program. Through research, you'll learn what your critical publics know and what they don't know.

Many superintendents today use networks of key public opinion leaders to take the pulse of their communities. Others use communication audits, which take a snapshot of a district's communication efforts and highlight gaps between perception and reality. Still others use "dipstick" research methods: they quickly measure single issues with selected audiences like PreK parents and ask them whether they would be willing to pay tuition for PreK classes. Some superintendents ask building staff to track and categorize calls received during the past month so they can get a picture of people's questions or concerns.

All these techniques help your communication effort develop messages that will lead to better understanding of and support for your schools.

Taking Action: Use Key
Opinion Leader Networks

Suppose you worked with your local TV station and gave them everything they asked for during an interview. You also spent hours researching and providing even more information for them. The subject of the interview was your school lunch program and its nutritional value as it relates to the youth obesity problem plaguing the country. Now your spouse has just called to report that the station will begin airing a three-part series on your lunch program that same evening. Knowing what you gave the reporters, you feel confident that the report will be at least balanced because of all the time and information you provided.

Wrong! The first report that evening was a disaster. They reported on items that you clearly demonstrated were not true. So what could you do?

Faced with a similar situation, one very large Texas school district fired up its own network of key opinion leaders by the next morning and e-mailed the entire network copies of documents that had been provided to the TV station to demonstrate how the media blatantly lied in their report. The unexpected result was that the city's movers and shakers rallied behind the school district and ignited such a firestorm that the station cancelled the remaining two segments.

Such is the power of a well-established key opinion network. *If you can put in place only one major communication tactic, make it a key opinion leader network.* A strong network includes many of the community's major influential leaders; other members may hold official leadership positions in service clubs, government agencies, business agencies, and so forth.

The best way to start a network is to invite groups of 10 to 12 leaders to meet with you to discuss their perceptions of your schools and to ask questions; your aim is to begin building face-to-face relationships and (you hope) trust with these leaders. Ask them to complete a database directory that you can use to send them e-mail updates and invitations to future meetings. Be open and regularly seek their opinions through e-mail newsletters or simple surveys. Ask them to call you if they hear rumors about your system.

Begin building a list of from 50 to 500 people, depending on the size of your system. I have never seen this tactic—if it's conducted in an open fashion—fail for a school system of any size. But once again, it takes action and your commitment to make it happen.

Taking Action: Putting Technology to Work for You

Technology is greatly changing how we communicate. Today's parents and leaders are conditioned to receive information faster than we can normally give it to them. Consequently, most effective communication efforts are now database-driven, allowing key messages to be sent to selected audiences in less than 30 minutes. For some parents, even that may be too slow—their child has already text-messaged them about the lockdown at their school.

But it is imperative to use the latest technology to help target and quickly disseminate your messages. Leading school districts are using services to send phone and e-mail messages to all students, parents, and staff. In times of crisis, you must have the capability to reach your entire school district family as fast as possible.

Leading superintendents know to get the right messages to the right people at the right times—and they know to deliver those messages with lightning speed. These superintendents create an infrastructure for communication that enables their district to reach key constituents within a 30- to 60-minute time frame.

Some questions offered by NSPRA member Nora Carr include the following:

> *Leading superintendents know to get the right messages to the right people at the right times—and they know to deliver those messages with lightning speed.*

- Do you have a database with complete contact information for community opinion leaders that includes business, politics, government, faith community, cultural institutions, advocacy groups, philanthropic groups, and nonprofit organizations? Do you have an e-delivery system to reach these leaders?
- Do you have a system for notifying all employees and all parents by multiple methods simultaneously and within minutes?
- When news breaks, can you post information on the district Web site and broadcast it on cable access television within minutes?
- Can your district quickly provide talking points and develop key messages for the leadership team, principals, and board?
- Do you have a bank of crisis messages and letters posted on a secure intranet or shared file that principals can access any time and adapt to communicate more effectively with parents?
- Can parents, employees, and other key constituents subscribe online to receive district news releases, emergency notifications, breaking news alerts, and other communications?

Taking Action: Blogging for Visibility

One of the more common responses we receive when completing a communications audit is that staff members want to see more of you, their system's leader. They want you to visit their building, see them in action, show support, and communicate the direction in which you see the district headed.

Even when superintendents make an extra effort to be visible, staff members in those schools not visited often feel that the superintendent may be clueless about what's really happening in their buildings. Sometimes these misguided feelings are based on the perception that you don't really care enough to know what's happening in the classrooms of your system. People tell us that if you cared, you would at least stop by once or twice a year to meet with them. And the peculiarity of this wish is that they expect the same contact with you whether you lead a system with 2,500 or 250,000 students.

Of course, most staff members and members of the community alike don't understand your job and how you actually spend your time. Recently, we came across a solution from both the school and corporate worlds that goes a long way toward curing this time-sapping dilemma, not only increasing visibility but also giving staff some insight into how you spend your time.

Dr. Chris Spence, the top administrator for the Hamilton–Wentworth District in Hamilton, Ontario, Canada, has periodically used a feature called "The Director's Place" on the system's Web site. It gives staff and others an opportunity to learn about his perception of the district and his visits to the schools through his "My Diary" page. This page is well done and even adds photos to accompany the annotated comments from the visits.

Most superintendents could create a periodic update of their visits to schools and businesses on their own internal Web sites or e-mail distribution systems. The point is to personalize it and demonstrate that you are connected to the staff, students, and communities you lead.

Once a month, think about running something like this online:

It's been a hectic month for many of us in the Nirvana Schools. But I was lucky enough to spend some time at Perfect High, and I can tell you that sitting in on Rosemary Boccella's AP English class reminded me of why I chose education as my profession many years ago. The kids were really into the class, and the discussion was something that I wish all our taxpayers could listen to because it proved just how well these kids think and write about today's issues.

As I was leaving Perfect High at the end of the day, I was struck by the huge number of students who were *not* leaving. They were actively engaged in clubs, the rehearsal for *The King and I,* plus all the spring sports practices and games scheduled for that day. Special kudos go to those staff members who devote their time to these activities for our kids as well.

Of course, this month had us finalizing next year's budget requests with the help of all our principals, attending the first meeting of the new e-mail/voicemail etiquette policy task force (headed by Tech Director Bob Responsive and composed of teachers, parents, and principals), and we are in the final round of yet another attendance area/boundary change due to the growth in our district.

So in some sense, it was business as usual for our schools, and I appreciate all that you do for the children of Nirvana.

Best Wishes

Remember, lack of communication creates a vacuum, and critics will rush in to fill it. Every administrator has a career-full of examples where critics have defined the issues before the school district has even started thinking about communication. You need to be transparent and proactive when it comes to your communication effort. Sometimes that means you might not have a lot to say in the early stages of an issue, but it does mean that you have to be first in defining the issue.

Remember, lack of communication creates a vacuum, and critics will rush in to fill it.

Doing something good and not letting anyone know about it is like winking in the dark. We need to get over the feeling that communicating great results should not be part of an educator's job. Most educators were taught to be humble and are not inclined to brag about their work. Consequently, too often members of the schools' various publics are treated only to negative news, partially because the good news is not being sent and used correctly.

Here's a quick tip: Use storytelling to communicate your good news. Don't say only that one of your high school students won the state essay contest on "What Democracy Means to Me." Explain that the winner could not speak English when she arrived in your system in fourth grade. Because of her determination, great home support, and excellent teachers, she now is one of the finest students in the district.

Good news is more than statistics. Tell stories about your students and staff to prove that your district is making your students—and your community—a success.

And in Closing . . .

Being successful as a superintendent will not happen if you don't make a commitment to communication. In one way, it's correct to say that no one person is responsible for all of your district's communication. Each employee has a major role in creating effective communication. But there is one person—the superintendent of schools—who sets the tone of commitment, openness, authenticity, and culture of communication for the entire district. Remember, when it comes to communication, you can never *not* lead. You are positioned to take action to make communication a powerful force for your entire school community.

REFERENCE

Schatz, K. (1986). *Managing by influence.* Upper Saddle River, NJ: Prentice Hall.

CHAPTER SIX

THE SUPERINTENDENT AS KEY COMMUNICATOR AND DIPLOMAT

A Case Study

DONALD A. PHILLIPS

Leaders of school districts inevitably face challenges that require clear communication and much diplomacy. This might include rolling out a new strategic direction, conveying information about budget reductions, dealing with social or political issues, or managing a disturbing set of events or even a tragedy. As school leaders, we are faced with many issues each and every year that require the most delicate balance of open, honest communication and diplomacy.

We school leaders talk a lot about the importance of strong communication, both within our school

Strong skills of communication and diplomacy come most into play when we face difficult and challenging circumstances.

community and with the broader public. We talk about the value of two-way communication and listening to our stakeholders. We talk about open and honest communication as a tool for building greater understanding and trust.

The notion of diplomacy, less often articulated, is a critical partner to communication and effective K–12 leadership. Diplomacy has its roots in building relationships with others to allow individuals within an organization or community to address challenging issues. An individual who demonstrates diplomacy is tactful and skilled at managing delicate situations. Therefore, strong skills of communication and diplomacy come most into play when we face difficult and challenging circumstances.

As school leaders, how can we best approach the difficult moments in our careers and not falter, but rather lead our organizations to be even stronger and more vital? This is no easy task. I'm hopeful that by drawing on my 18 years of experience as a superintendent, and focusing through the lens of a recent series of very troubling events in our school district, I can extract a series of lessons that I believe cut across the important challenges.

A NOOSE IS FOUND

In early October 2007, I was attending a statewide superintendents meeting over 400 miles away from our district when I received a phone call from the assistant superintendent and our communications director. They reported that a noose had been discovered after school the previous day, hanging in a boys' bathroom in one of our high schools. No message was attached to the noose, but the symbolism of a noose, the history of lynching in our nation, and racial hatred immediately bubbled up in my mind.

Our initial conversations centered on the details of the scene, potential leads, and reporting the incident to the local sheriff's office. The school was treating the incident as an internal disciplinary matter and an isolated event. There was some initial discussion from the school's leadership of whether the noose could somehow be connected with an attempted suicide or a call for help. From the principal's perspective, the less said the better, given fears about potential copycat acts, the possibility of increased tensions on campus among the races, and the danger of the high school's excellent reputation being tarnished by potential media coverage. As a former high school principal, I understood the principal's instinct to protect the school.

As the superintendent, however, I knew we could not and should not "circle the wagons." We needed to involve the sheriff; communicate our sense of outrage as a school community; and clearly state that acts of discrimination, prejudice, and hate would not be tolerated on our campuses. I understood that it was only a matter of time until the media picked up the story. As a superintendent, I have come to understand that there are no secrets, and that it is always better to act proactively rather than reactively.

Like the principal, I too wondered how such a disturbing event could happen in our district. I fretted over losing our focus on improving student achievement. However, I also saw an opportunity. As a school district, we had recently focused on increasing student achievement for all; as a by-product, less of our institutional time and energy had gone into directly attacking issues of diversity, tolerance, and understanding. Increasingly, I had come to realize that if our students were to be prepared for life in the 21st century, they were going to need not only strong academic skills but also the ability to successfully navigate and work collaboratively in a diverse world of different races, cultures, religions, regions, and ideas.

This unfortunate event provided us with a teachable moment to focus on the importance of differences, respect, and cultural competence. A crisis or major negative event can almost always be seen as either a problem or an opportunity. I was convinced that we needed to look on this very unfortunate occurrence as an opportunity.

By 11:30 on the same morning that I was first notified of the noose, news trucks were rolling into the district office parking lot to go live with the breaking story. A parent who heard of the story had called the local press in an effort to link her concerns regarding a disciplinary matter involving her child with this story, even though they were not connected. From the original call to the arrival of the media, we had had only a little more than an hour to frame the issue and support the principal in developing a statement to share with the media. I believed it essential that all messages to our students, staff, parents, and media from the principal and me should clearly state our disappointment and collective outrage. It was important to present a consistent message that such acts would not be tolerated and that this act was the antithesis of what we stand for as a school community.

By mid-afternoon, the principal had communicated what had happened, conveyed his belief in the school community, and reaffirmed the value of acceptance and tolerance to all students and staff. By the end of the school day, the entire high school parent community had received a similar message, both by phone and e-mail, through our school-to-home communication network.

It was important to present a consistent message that such acts would not be tolerated and that this act was the antithesis of what we stand for as a school community.

The story created some buzz in the broader community, but most saw it as an isolated event whose perpetrator may or may not have understood the full implications of the act. Our African American parents, however, felt deep concern, anger, and fear. An activist group of African American parents publicly shared their outrage in the local media and spoke at the next school board meeting. They saw a need for both the school and the district to take stronger action immediately. This event became a lightning rod for long-standing concerns in our African American community regarding cultural competence, diversity training for students and staff, the need for more African American teachers, and concerns about the achievement gap.

TWO MORE INCIDENTS

A few weeks later, on Halloween, a student at another high school in our district wore to school what he said was a ghost costume, but it looked very much like a Ku Klux Klan outfit. A teacher and then an administrator shared their perceptions with the student and asked him to remove the outfit. The student removed the costume but put it back on during the lunch period and paraded in front of a group of African American students—many of whom, ironically, were his friends.

This story also quickly hit the airwaves, with competing views voiced across the political spectrum of talk shows and news agencies about the intent and about what disciplinary measures, if any, would be appropriate. The student claimed that he did not understand the hurtful nature of his actions; he had been certain, he said, that his friends would see his costume as somehow humorous. The internal and external debates picked up steam and visibility around whether these two incidents were isolated acts born out of ignorance, insensitivity, and stupidity, or whether they represented deeper patterns of hatred and racism.

Only a week later, at yet another of our district high schools, a noose was found hanging over the doorway of a stage set for the school play *A Streetcar Named Desire,* in which two African American students played the lead roles of Stanley and Blanche. In addition, a nearby hand-painted sign containing racial epithets was brought to the attention of the drama teacher and administrators. After an initial investigation, a student quickly came forward to admit to asking another student to tie a hangman's noose, saying he did not understand the full implications of his actions or how hurtful they would be to the two student actors, as well as to other African American students. Again, the media immediately aired the story.

The interpretation of these incidents—whether they were the result of insensitive or copycat acts and how much racism and hatred drove the acts—continued to differ throughout the community.

TAKING THE LARGER VIEW AND BEING ON POINT

As superintendent, I knew that these incidents could not be delegated to others to handle. I worked with the school principals and senior district staff members to ensure that appropriate disciplinary action was taken and that our school sites developed appropriate site-based interventions to turn these terrible events into learning opportunities.

After the first noose incident, we brought together all administrators in our district to clarify what had happened, to share my expectations and those of the district, and to ask our administrators to engage staff in responding to the initial event and its implications as they worked with students. It was essential for everyone to know where I stood, and where we all needed to stand together, around the issue of providing a welcoming environment for all, as well as the need to be absolutely clear that harassing or threatening acts of prejudice, discrimination, or hate would not be tolerated. We talked together about the symbolism of our roles as site and district leaders and the fact that what each leader says or does will set the tone for the site. As a result, individual school sites and departments engaged students and staff in discussions, using upcoming diversity assemblies or school events as opportunities to reaffirm collective school commitments to tolerance, diversity, and respect.

When the next two incidents occurred, the clarity of direction coming out of this districtwide meeting, as well as the learnings that resulted from the first incident, prepared the high school principals to be proactive immediately and to turn these disturbing events into learning opportunities that could help to build a more resilient learning community for all. For example, students at one of the high schools almost immediately made a DVD to be shared schoolwide, using student voices on diversity and tolerance and the need to "take back" their high school. They also printed T-shirts celebrating diversity in an effort to reaffirm where the school stands. The positive response by the overall student body strengthened the sense of community while teaching important life lessons around complex issues of race.

These three events convinced me that, at a minimum, we had major work to do in building cultural and racial sensitivity and that I needed to reach out more directly to our parents and community. While some continued to argue that these were isolated events, I realized that if I myself did not hold a series of courageous conversations with our parents and community, I would have lost an opportunity to turn these incidents into teachable moments to move our organization forward around a host of issues regarding diversity and race. I further ran the risk of "enabling" future acts by not taking on these events more directly as superintendent.

———————— ✂ ————————

I realized that if I myself did not hold a series of courageous conversations with our parents and community, I would have lost an opportunity to turn these incidents into teachable moments to move our organization forward.

Knowing when to let a building principal carry the day and when to step in as a superintendent is always a difficult call. It had become increasingly clear, as each incident occurred, that a more visible districtwide response was not only appropriate but also absolutely necessary. As the system's leader, I needed to be clear with students, staff, parents, and community about where we stood as a school district.

My conclusion prompted me to send an e-mail to all staff titled, "I'm Deeply Troubled." At the same time, our district office sent an e-mail communication to all parents districtwide (with a printed letter mailed to families who did not have e-mail addresses) stating how seriously we treat such matters and asking parents to talk with their children in an age-appropriate way regarding their understanding of differences, tolerance, and respect.

While the reaction to my letter was largely muted, some felt that it made a mountain out of a molehill, others thought the letter was on point but they also called for an immediate plan of aggressive action, and still others felt that both my tone and message were on target. I realized that I couldn't please everybody, but the communication to staff and parents left no question about where I stood as superintendent, what we valued as a school district, and what would not be tolerated. I needed to be very clear that a response of "I did not understand the implications of my actions" would not be acceptable and would not hold any sway in terms of the severity of the consequences. I further wanted to surface concerns about less overt forms of racism and have us as a school community address subtler forms of prejudice, intolerance, and discrimination.

These deeply disturbing events created a forum that allowed us to address deeper issues that would have been harder to confront without the visibility and urgency surrounding this series of events. It was also important to start to broaden the conversation beyond race alone to include issues of diversity and respect around religion, ethnic and cultural backgrounds, social and political beliefs, sexual orientation, and the importance of developing respect for differences as a key 21st-century life skill.

GOING DEEPER

I realized that our districtwide communications were at most a good first step, but were far from bringing closure to the matter. As a next step at the senior staff level, we began an exhaustive review of our board policy on harassment and hate behavior. While we had little time prior to the upcoming board meeting, we recognized the importance and urgency of moving quickly to place this issue on the very next agenda. As we reviewed district policy, we recognized that it lacked a sense of moral imperative and was more technical and procedural in nature. We thought about what was important to be included in the policy and reviewed policies from other comparable districts as well as policy guidelines from the California School Boards Association.

As the new policy quickly took shape, we involved principals, assistant principals, and other key personnel in the process to obtain feedback on the policy and the accompanying administrative procedures. I wanted both their input and, ultimately, their buy-in, since they would have to bring any changes to life at the school-site level. From a systems perspective, the board policy and procedures would serve as the launching pad for future action, student and staff training, curriculum development, disciplinary action, and hiring practices.

A little more than 2 months after the initial incident, we presented to the school board a completely rewritten board policy with administrative procedures on harassment and hate behavior. As the board meeting moved forward and the local news cameras rolled, the sense of anger and hurt by the African American community was unmistakable and understandable. They wanted clear and strong steps to be taken against the perpetrators, no matter the circumstances or context. School board members clearly stated their sense of urgency in addressing the matter, their personal disappointment that such incidents could take place in our school district, and their support for the new policy and procedures.

It would take us 2 more months to further refine the administrative procedures. We met with our African American community. We also met with the Latino community, our Human Relations District Advisory Committee, the gay and lesbian community, and student groups to seek input and refine our procedures. Over the course of the discussions, the emphasis changed—for all parties—from a focus on harsh consequences to education aimed at creating a school and district climate of understanding differences and respect. When the board took action on the policy and procedures, only a few speakers came forward to address the board, and all spoke about the positive direction that was growing out of our joint efforts.

Lessons Learned

Drawing from this case study and a full range of personal experiences as a superintendent, I believe there are a number of lessons for system leaders about communication and diplomacy that can be applied in any challenging or difficult situation. I suggest the following:

Lesson 1—Be open, honest, and proactive. It is essential that system leaders be forthright in our communications. Being open and honest might seem risky at first, but it is also disarming. It allows a leader to be proactive in managing the situation by helping frame the issue and the responses to action. Even more important, it builds trust in your organization and leadership. If one is perceived as telling only part of the story or covering up an important matter, trust is almost immediately lost. Being open, honest, and proactive sends a message that no matter how difficult an issue is at the time, we are going to address it directly and keep our community in the know. Even if portions of the community disagree with the proposed next steps—and they will—stating your position openly and honestly will foster better communication and is more likely to lead to a positive resolution.

Lesson 2—Listen carefully and do not be afraid to modify your course. While we need to be open, honest, and proactive communicators, we also need to be deep listeners who are willing to make midcourse adjustments. As system leaders, we need not only to share our views, but also to listen to the different perspectives of others. Sometimes opposing views may be self-serving or at odds with the fundamental tenets of our public school systems; in other instances, however, they may bring a fresh or divergent point of view that warrants our attention and possible adjustments to our plans.

Furthermore, we need to avoid the trap of "Damn the torpedoes, full speed ahead." When the issue becomes about power or winning versus losing, we lose the moral high ground as leaders of our organization. We need to be mature enough as leaders to acknowledge when appropriate changes should be made in response to divergent points of view that have merit.

Lesson 3—Turn challenges into opportunities. The most difficult times can also serve as opportunities for learning and growth, both as system leaders and within organizations. Often our first instinct is to think of how we can manage a difficult situation and minimize collateral damage. In some instances this makes good sense, in order to keep the focus on the district's primary learning mission or to avoid being overwhelmed with too many side issues at once. The more difficult and challenging the issue, however, the more likely it is to require greater attention. Such situations present opportunities for an organization to learn and grow; they can serve as "teachable moments" for all. As system leaders, we need to be thoughtful about picking from the challenges we face daily to select the right ones and turn them into opportunities for learning and growth, both professionally and organizationally.

> *During challenging times, it is essential to stand up and be counted for what we value as system leaders and what we believe is the right thing to do—even if it is not the most popular position. . . . Leadership, in its most difficult hour, is taking a divergent path.*

Lesson 4—Be on point. During challenging times, it is essential to stand up and be counted for what we value as system leaders and what we believe is the right thing to do—even if it is not the most popular position. Leadership can involve building a consensus or determining where the herd is headed and jumping in front. Leadership, in its most difficult hour, is taking a divergent path. This involves doing what we believe is right, even if it entails rough sailing. This is where relationship building and diplomacy become critical skills. As system leaders in public institutions, we cannot single-handedly muscle through an unpopular proposal of any significance. We need to build understanding and reframe the issue if we are to lead a sufficient majority to be prepared to take a different tack. The ability to articulate a clear message and rationale and to build internal and external coalitions can only happen when the system leader is on point. The caution here is not to get too far ahead of the organization and your internal and external constituencies so that you lose the ability to serve as their leader.

Lesson 5—Think systemically and keep your eye on the vision. As a superintendent, the clearer your vision and the stronger the district's strategic plan, the easier it will be to determine the issues to heed as opportunities for organizational growth. The key is to think systemically about the organization by looking for patterns and opportunities that others most likely will not see at first. This is where it is critical to be able to stand on the "balcony" to allow deeper reflection and a loftier perspective about what is transpiring. Viewing all sides of an issue and seeing the connection with the broader organization can only happen if we detach ourselves from the emotional daily turmoil of being on the front line. The ability to see both the forest *and* the trees in challenging times can be very difficult, but it is critical to being an effective leader who keeps his or her organization moving forward.

Lesson 6—Be transparent. Our work as system leaders in public schools has become increasingly public. Establishing a culture of transparency in terms of what goes on in our school systems—being open about "the good, the bad, and the ugly" and how we are proceeding to make a difference—is increasingly essential to a system leader's success. Distrust and questions about intentions will follow if issues go public without ongoing, forthcoming leadership. In so many situations that go awry, the "process" becomes the issue. Being transparent makes it less likely people will challenge or criticize the process. It must be recognized that not all situations will go public, and sometimes we are sure to be surprised by what is picked up or missed. However, to hope that a big issue will just go away is playing Russian roulette when the stakes are high and your credibility as a leader is on the line.

Lesson 7—Follow through with commitments. Challenging times require delicate communication and diplomacy to set the tone and direction. This is just the beginning, however, as we need to make good on our promises and commitments. Otherwise, our credibility and integrity are at risk. These are reflected not by what we *say* we are going to do, but *what we actually do*. As system leaders, it is our responsibility to keep our commitments center stage and act consistently in alignment with our beliefs and values, even after the heat of the moment dies down. Otherwise, we undermine our most important assets as leaders: our credibility, trustworthiness, and integrity.

Concluding Thoughts

The superintendent is uniquely positioned to serve as the key communicator and diplomat for his or her school district. If as leaders we are thoughtful and strategic about how we use these key skills, we can be more successful as leaders and, more importantly, we can help ensure the long-term viability of our organizations through continuous improvement and growth.

CHAPTER SEVEN

THE SUPERINTENDENT AS BLOGGER

MARK J. STOCK

"Not me! Absolutely not me!" stammered Randy, my friend and colleague. The discussion at the superintendents meeting had turned to blogging. "I get enough criticism as it is. I don't need another wacko taking pot shots at me from left field on the Internet," he added, wincing as he said it. "Why should I provide an easy forum for another critic?"

"Randy, don't you think the rational folks in your school district recognize a wacko when they hear one?" I responded.

"Yeah, most of them probably do, but I still don't want to lie awake at night wondering what the next critic is posting," he responded.

"Do you lie awake now?" I asked with a smirk.

"Well . . . sure! Doesn't every superintendent do that occasionally?" he asked. "I just don't want to make it easier for people like that to have a voice."

"I hear you," I acknowledged, "but what you don't realize is that now *every* person has a voice if they want to be heard. The explosion of online communication through blogging, Web sites, chat rooms, instant messaging, e-mails, and even text messaging means that every Tom, Dick, and Harry has a voice if they want one. The modern, tech-savvy superintendent recognizes that he or she had better have a technological forum established *before* the wackos show up.

"What's more," I continued, "if you have an Internet presence that's popular, educational, and already established, your rational public will bury your wackos when they do show up. Most of the folks we represent get embarrassed by people like that who try to represent your community!"

"I don't know, Mark," Randy sighed. "I think my skin is too thin and my head is too thick to learn how to blog!"

I chuckled sympathetically, then added, "Maybe you'd better start blogging *to* them before they start blogging *about* you!"

He shrugged his shoulders and sighed. "You can't teach an old dog new tricks. I lasted this long; I can make it a few more years."

"You might survive," I said, "but the new superintendent is expected to *thrive,* not just survive. Blogging is one more potential tool in the toolbox of the modern school superintendent."

—————— ✀ ——————

One of the most important benefits of blogging for the school administrator comes from interacting with the community.

"Well, just consider me 'old school,' then," he said with a grin.

I nodded and replied, "'Old school' I can understand, but while you're sipping margaritas in an RV park in Arizona, our younger colleagues are going to be on the front lines. Who knows what challenges they'll face? If we don't find new ways of getting the good word out about public education, the term 'old school' might mean more than you think!"

As the meeting ended and we went our separate ways, I wondered once again what the future would hold for superintendents on the front lines of the war on public education.

SO WHAT'S A BLOG?

The term *blog* is still relatively new, and like most new technological terms, you probably won't find it in your spell checker yet. The word *blog* comes from combining the words "Web" (short for World Wide Web) and "log" (an ongoing record of events or activities). A blog, therefore, is a Web site that is updated regularly with a variety of content. Blogging is the act of journaling on a regular basis on the Internet. A blogger is the person posting the main information found on the site.

The types of blogs available on the Web are limited only by the imagination of the bloggers. There are political blogs, technology blogs, family blogs, sports blogs, quilting blogs, homemaker blogs, school blogs, teacher blogs, and even satire blogs. If you have thought about it, then someone is blogging about it. These blogs can be open to everyone to read, or open only to those invited by the blogger. Blogs can be open to commentary or closed to reader comments. They can be open to comment only on selected postings or open on every posting. You can even set up your blog to approve comments *before* they are posted. Many options are available to the blogger, depending on the purpose and scope of the blog. However, the one thing that all good blogs have in common is that they post a variety of content on a frequent basis.

HOW IS BLOGGING DIFFERENT?

One of the most important benefits of blogging for the school administrator comes from interacting with the community. While most Web sites are fairly static (and, in many cases, even out of date), successful blog sites are updated frequently—often daily, or several times a day. Why? When patrons log on to the site, they expect to see something new. The existence of new material actually reinforces frequent visits to the site. A patron who accesses a site two or three times and does not find new information is less likely to return. Most successful bloggers allow visitors to leave comments, making it highly likely that a frequent visitor will find something new, even if it is only found in the comment sections of the blog.

The interaction among visitors who leave comments is one of the features that distinguish blogs from other Web sites. When the moderator of a blog allows visitors to interact by discussing their opinions and reactions to the postings, the result is a vibrant online community that not only attracts more visitors but also encourages more frequent visits to the site. Those "wackos" my friend Randy was worrying about are actually one of the magnetic forces that pulls visitors to a site. Just because you've never before heard that out-in-left-field voice doesn't mean that it hasn't always existed. Many rational people are actually shocked to find out that there really are people with unusual points of view.

The daily posting of new content and the interaction of online readers are two of the main features that distinguish a blog site from traditional school Web sites.

Why Do People Blog?

People blog for many reasons, but two of the most compelling are to gain a wider forum for their thoughts and to connect with other people interested in the same subjects. Even young people blog. While the young have always wanted to leave their mark on the world, the advent of blogging software has created an easy-to-use forum that allows them to have a worldwide soapbox to stand on.

Do you remember as a youth when you sought to leave your mark on the world by carving your initials into the tree in your backyard? Or remember when you dragged your stick through the wet cement in the new sidewalk, leaving a message for all who passed by? Well, our children and grandchildren are seeking to leave their mark electronically. They use social networking and blogging software to post their thoughts and views for the world to see. And, just like the initials in the tree or the words on the sidewalk that seemed to last forever, so too do the digital footprints left by today's new generations seem to last. So how does this trend affect the educational leader?

If You Can't Beat 'em, Join 'em!

First of all, blogging is not going to go away. In our world today, if educational leaders don't blog, then it's just a matter of time before others will blog about them. In many communities across the country, the superintendent of schools and the school principal are the most public figures. People in the community expect them to have a public persona and to present a professional and transparent face.

In today's world, blogging provides a ready-made public forum. I maintain that since you can't beat 'em, you might as well join 'em.

In today's world, blogging provides a ready-made public forum. I maintain that since you can't beat 'em, you might as well join 'em. I once received an e-mail from a woman on the East Coast who wanted me to see her Web log. I clicked on the hyperlink she provided in her e-mail and was surprised to find a blog that was solely dedicated to an attempt to fire the superintendent of her school district. Each day she would blog to the community an ongoing attack on the superintendent's philosophies and practices.

The old-school mantra was, "Never argue with those who buy their ink by the barrel!" I maintain that the new mantra is, "Everyone has a barrel of ink, so you'd better have one too!"

CONNECTING WITH THE COMMUNITY—OLD SCHOOL

The old-school educational leader who wanted to connect with the community was usually known for hanging out at the Friday night ball games and chatting up the crowd. While attending these events is still an expectation in most school communities, the savvy school leader has realized that this crowd does not represent the entire community.

Being physically present is not always possible for either the patrons or the school administrator. So technology-minded school leaders are supplementing their old-school political presence with a new tool called the blog. When the leader has established a regular Internet presence, he or she is able to speak to a much wider audience. This audience is often a much more diverse community than those reached in traditional school venues.

CONNECTING WITH THE COMMUNITY—NEW SCHOOL

Blogging provides a forum to reach patrons who may be unreachable in conventional forums. Most of the power brokers and taxpayers in many local communities are aging baby boomers who no longer have children (or maybe even grandchildren) in the schools. One result of our highly mobile society is that many retired people have no personal ties to any individuals in their local schools. These folks may never get to know the school leaders or the issues that plague their school system, at least through the conventional forums on which school leaders have typically relied.

As a former superintendent whose Web log was widely read, I found it interesting that a few of my most frequent readers and personal supporters were retired individuals in the community whom I would meet in the local fitness center. These individuals had no family in the area but had chosen to retire on one of the tourist lakes popular in the region. They would chat frequently with me while jogging on the treadmills. The topics often centered on subjects I had blogged about that week. Though they had no family members in the school district, still they were significant taxpayers in the community. Their only sources of information about schools were through the newspaper and my blog.

School leaders frequently make the mistake of thinking that the patrons they see at traditional school events actually represent the entire community. It doesn't take long as a blogging school leader to recognize that there are multiple voices and multiple views on virtually every issue. Leaders who allow patrons to leave comments on their daily blogs will soon recognize the wide diversity of opinion that exists within any community.

ADVANTAGES OF BLOGGING

You control your message. One of the greatest advantages to blogging as a school leader is that you control the central message. You run no risk of being misquoted. If it comes out wrong, it's entirely your fault. And you don't have to depend on others to get your message out. This approach isn't for the faint of heart, of course, because there's no one else to blame!

While your central message is controlled through your regular postings on the blog site, you don't always control the public's reaction to those postings unless you choose to. The superintendent may control even the responses to his or her blog by requiring all comments to be approved before posting or by not allowing any comments. These decisions are entirely under the control of the blog moderator. Like most things, of course, there are benefits and drawbacks to both options.

You can respond to traditional media. A commonly expressed frustration of school leaders is the occasional occurrence of inaccurate or misleading stories printed in the local newspapers. The leader with a regular blog and a dependable readership can instantly make a correction or respond to inaccurate reports published in traditional media outlets.

The normal response of the school leader is to fire off a letter to the newspaper editor, explaining or correcting perceived inaccuracies. The problem is that by the time the letter to the editor is published, the readers may not remember the original article that prompted it. Or perhaps they never got around to reading it at all. With many newspapers now publishing online versions of their newspapers and archiving them, the tech-savvy superintendent can write a response to an offending article on his or her blog and then hyperlink (insert a Web link) to the original article (also on the blog) so the public can refer to it. In addition, the superintendent could write a traditional letter to the editor for the hard-copy version of the newspaper and then refer the public to the blog site for a complete review of the story.

The message is asynchronous—you don't have to be present to win! A great advantage of the technology of blogging is that it is asynchronous, meaning that things don't have to happen in chronological order. In our busy world, school patrons are on the go continually. With so many activities and events going on, school supporters are not always able to attend school board meetings and conventional communication events that occur in real time. The local newspaper may

Perhaps one of the most unusual and counterintuitive things I found as a blogging superintendent is that the traditional media outlets actually read my blog and contacted me more frequently for interviews.

already be lining the bottom of the bird cage by the time some citizens get around to thinking of reading the article explaining the new building project.

Accessing announcements and daily postings through a blog site allows everyone to keep up with such issues. The archiving feature of blogging software even allows patrons to search your entire blog site by entering search terms for the topics they're interested in. Any postings you've made on this topic will instantly pop up, allowing busy readers to determine what your take was on this issue. This asynchronous feature is very useful in today's busy world. Another bonus is that searching the archives is a lot less messy than dragging the newspaper out from the bottom of the bird cage!

Blogs increase coverage in traditional media. Perhaps one of the most unusual and counterintuitive things I found as a blogging superintendent is that the traditional media outlets actually read my blog and contacted me more frequently for interviews. My first thought when I started blogging was that newspapers would feel threatened and that journalists would not seek my opinion as often because I would have my own forum for releasing information. I found the opposite to be true. I found that numerous journalists, especially those who cover educational issues exclusively, were frequent blog readers who scoured the Web regularly looking for potential story ideas. They frequently called to seek my opinion on a variety of issues. This also increased the positive exposure of the school district in traditional media outlets.

Blogs build a sense of community. The online environment builds a sense of community among regular readers. The wise leader never overlooks an opportunity to take advantage of these opportunities for community building. One very important part of this blogging network is that it often brings a sense of community to people who are not always in the normal network of school events.

This concept hit home forcibly one week when a patron sent me a private e-mail acknowledging how much she felt a part of our school system since reading my blog. In the e-mail she left her name. After inquiring with our principals, I learned a little more about her. She was a parent with two special-needs children, living in a small trailer park. She had very little formal education and had minimal income, but she had an Internet connection and she used it to stay on top of school activities and issues. In her e-mail she admitted that she felt too intimidated to call or stop by my office, but she felt brave enough to talk to the superintendent through anonymous blog comments and e-mail. This emphasized for me once again that every community is full of people who care, but who often feel too intimidated to make their opinions known in more traditional ways. The sense of community that can occur in online environments can be very powerful.

Think about the relationships you're building behind the scenes when hundreds and even thousands of people are reading your postings and daily musings. If you're doing your job well, these readers will soon develop a feel for who you are and what you represent through these daily postings.

WAYS TO USE A BLOG

Blogging has some clear advantages and benefits, and there are numerous ways to realize them. The following list outlines a variety of ways in which school leaders can use blogging to their advantage.

Spread the news. Perhaps the simplest and most common way of getting started on accessing the benefits of blogging is to use your Web log as an electronic newsletter. The PR-savvy leader will take all items typically released in a traditional newsletter and simply cut and paste them, including pictures, into the Web log. This is a quick, cheap, easy way to release a variety of information.

As a blogging superintendent, I would frequently announce the results of various athletic events or post the decisions from the previous evening's school board meeting. In communities with active local media and daily newspapers, this process can be even simpler. When local newspapers have carried online coverage of school events, the blogging school leader can simply hyperlink to the articles that are already on the Web and include any talking points or clarifications.

Communicating during an emergency. One of the most helpful ways of communicating important information during an emergency is to use the blog site. Snow delays, snow cancellations, power outages, bomb threats, and other emergencies can be chronicled online through the leader's Web log. The advantage of using the blog to update the public in an emergency is that the information is available online as soon as the patron accesses the site. With traditional media such as radio and television, the patron is not always able to access the information immediately.

Another advantage is that use of the blog can free up busy phone lines by taking away at least some of the telephone traffic. One year when I was a superintendent, we had a lockdown procedure in process at a local school due to a potential gun threat. When patrons found out about the lockdown, they immediately began calling the school. School personnel referred them immediately to my Web log. On my blog I detailed the chronology of the event and indicated that everyone was safe and that as soon as the situation was resolved I would post immediately. The site received thousands of hits during the short crisis. Local school patrons knew where to go to get the most current and accurate information. After the crisis, I received many posts thanking me for publishing the information and keeping everyone informed.

On another occasion, there was an accident involving a school bus in which the driver of another vehicle was killed. Upon arriving at the hospital, I immediately accessed a computer in the waiting area and blogged an update, indicating that all the students were currently safe and in good condition. I also used the blog to announce the procedures we would use for releasing students to their parents from the hospital.

Students and parents are now accustomed to this type of instantaneous communication. Whenever the school leader can provide this same level of communication, it is generally appreciated by most of the community.

Blogging the incident "live" from the hospital gave my Web log heightened legitimacy as a forum for current and accurate information. It also reinforced the importance of this forum and brought new readers to the site. By the time I got to the accident site, most of the students had already text-messaged their families, called them via cell phone, and even e-mailed pictures to their friends from those same cell phones. As a result, a handful of parents were already waiting outside the buses. Students and parents are now accustomed to this type of instantaneous communication. Whenever the school leader can provide this same level of communication, it is generally appreciated by most of the community.

Monitoring ongoing events. Using a Web log is a great way to monitor progress of an ongoing project or event in your school district. John Hill, a former superintendent and colleague of mine, used his blog ("The Plymouth Truth") to make regular progress reports on construction projects. Weekly updates, including reports on road closures and other issues, kept readers informed of the project's status. Any ongoing event that requires a regular updating of information for the public may provide good blogging material.

One of the most practical examples of the use of a Web log to monitor ongoing events is in chronicling the weather issues that plague some districts. On those mornings when snowfall and icy conditions threatened us with school closings, the traffic to my blog site would increase substantially. It was not uncommon on snowy days for my Web log to have 5,000 hits before 6 AM!

Incidentally, on days when the blog gets high traffic, it's important for the educational leader to use such opportunities to educate the public on other issues of importance to the school district. I routinely saved important but not necessarily time-sensitive postings in draft mode and held them until high-traffic occasions occurred. By releasing these posts when readership is high and Internet traffic is at a maximum, the educational leader is maximizing the opportunity to share important information or ideas.

One of the most memorable days I ever experienced was a high-traffic day. It was a snowy, nasty winter morning, and Internet traffic to the site was already high as community members and parents monitored the site to see if the 2-hour snow delay would be changed to a cancellation due to deteriorating weather conditions. When I didn't announce a cancellation, the comments turned angry. A few patrons considered the decision to hold school to be a mistake, and that's putting it mildly! When they took a few potshots at me on the comment section of the blog, several other patrons signed on to defend me. One of the defenders made a snide comment about "stay-at-home" moms whining on the Internet and told them to "go bake some cookies or something." Very soon the interchanges resembled the *Jerry Springer Show,* and the patrons were slinging mud at each other. While it was mostly comical, I eventually shut off the comments when they reached 119 and froze that portion of the site so that no more comments could be made on that posting. There were over 71,000 hits on the site that day—it was the talk of the town everywhere I went. As I walked the halls of the high school, the students smiled knowingly at me, making it clear that even they were reading my blog and talking about it.

The critical point here is that it takes only a few of these types of days to drive community awareness of a leader's Web log to higher levels. Such days are not common occurrences for the blogging leader, and they are usually uncomfortable. But one unusual (and useful) side effect is that they tend to increase traffic and obtain new readers. Most school leaders shy away from such perceived negativity, but for the most part issues like these are harmless and do bring about more interest in the blog site.

Blogging is a contact sport, and those with thin skin probably won't appreciate it. My personal experience is that such occurrences as the above are often caused by students posing as adults online and enjoying the spectacle of watching adults weigh into the fray and take their inflammatory comments seriously. After the incident I just described occurred, an employee stopped by my office to let me know that her own high school–age children had been observed clustered around the computer with their friends, posing as adults and posting anonymous comments.

Again, in my own experience, in almost every case of these types of outbreaks of negativity, it happened on a snowy day when there was a large increase in the number of students monitoring the blog site in the hopes that school would be canceled or delayed. The solution to this temporary "crisis" was to shut off comments on the postings regarding weather delays. The positive side to what happened, however, is that it brought thousands of new readers to the site as my blog became the talk of the town.

Being an activist. Every school leader knows that being an advocate and an activist for public education is a critical part of a leader's role. Being politically active is not only a professional obligation but in many communities is absolutely expected of the leader by the school board.

There are traditional ways in which leaders can be involved in this political function through professional associations at the state and national levels. However, there is also a growing need for community activism at the grassroots level. Think about the potential impact on the political scene if every superintendent in America had an active and growing readership on his or her local blog site. In many small communities, the local superintendent is the closest thing they have to a local political figure. Imagine how quickly important messages could be distributed, for instance, when a legislative bill in the state or local government is introduced.

On my blog site, I placed a small "sticker" on the sidebar that allowed a patron to e-mail his or her legislator. This sticker was a small piece of Java-script code that permitted patrons to type in their zip code and then their street address. This not only gave them the names and contact information for all their state and national political representatives, but it also gave them a pop-up screen that allowed them to instantly type an e-mail message to their legislator. This made political activism on educational issues as simple as a few mouse clicks and the typing of a short message.

One state legislator told me that he stacked up all the form letters from the lobbyists and their associations in one big pile and considered them as a single letter. Then he looked at all the private e-mails and personal letters, stacked them up, and considered them individually. Obviously he placed great importance on the opinions of separate individuals who were part of his constituency.

Think about how powerful it would be if even a third of your blog readers sent their legislator an e-mail telling their opinion on a piece of legislation. The grassroots activism on educational issues would increase tremendously. Legislators are not often accustomed to hearing from many individual patrons.

Marketing and PR. School leaders are increasingly aware of the need to market our schools. The privatization of schools and the increased variety of public and private school choices have resulted in a heightened awareness of the need to spread the good news about public schools.

> *A blogging school leader with a faithful readership will find regular opportunities to share a school district's positive attributes.*

A blogging school leader with a faithful readership will find regular opportunities to share a school district's positive attributes. The tech-savvy school leader can share video clips from ball games, or post graphs and audio blogs explaining the latest district test scores that were released in the newspapers. Any or all of these kinds of items can be integrated into a multimedia look and feel that will use the strengths of the Internet.

People in the community want to be part of what's happening. They want to be in the know. When folks explain at the office how they heard about it on the school superintendent's Web log, that news will get around the community—and your readership will grow.

Though schools have not followed the traditional business model of marketing their products, school people have a long track record of successfully promoting schools. The successful school leader will continue to use traditional PR methods but will also use the blog site and other modern tools. All press releases or newspaper articles may be used as blog material in addition to being promoted via traditional media outlets.

Getting to know you. How does a person who has never met you get to know you? With the Internet, it is now possible to feel a sense of connection to people you've never met face-to-face.

Once I received a private e-mail from a patron expressing her thankfulness that I was not all about "power," but that I was willing to talk to people through my Web log. She said she felt like she knew me, though she had never met me. This sense of authenticity helps people catch important glimpses of who the leader really is—and that builds trust.

I was told once that the reason my blog site worked was that I didn't write to people in "superintendent memo mode." For example, on Fridays I ran a regular feature called "Friday's Funnies" in which I told funny stories about kids. Many readers told me that they often logged onto my site on Friday just to get a chuckle for the day. And while they were there, of course, they scrolled down through the postings to see what else I was rambling about that week. Showing a sense of humor is a critical part of letting the community know who you are.

Another way of connecting personally with your readers is to tell about a vacation you went on, or about your hobbies and what you do for fun. This shows that even the superintendent is a real human being, and that's part of what helps us see our leaders as approachable and normal. On occasion, I'd refer to my children and use examples of routine family life that would help readers feel like they knew a little more about me.

Educating the community. Perhaps one of the most useful purposes of your blog site is to use it as a teaching tool. Educational leaders often find themselves making decisions that appear at best confusing and at worst hypocritical to members of the local community. The reason for that, of course, is that leaders often have information and knowledge that may not be readily available or apparent to local patrons.

The use of a Web log is an excellent way of informing and educating the public on urgent or politically important matters. The best method is to dole out such information in small doses in daily or weekly postings. This not only allows readers the opportunity to digest the information, but it also provides a method of reviewing the information over time without appearing to talk down to your readers.

Some very complex issues can be explained to the public quite successfully through a blog. I frequently blogged about the complexities of property taxes to our local patrons. Due to the large number of lakefront properties, our school district had some of the highest assessed property values in the state, and yet the school district's per-pupil revenues were low. Explaining this disconnect to local patrons was always a challenge. Individuals would open their property tax bills and assume that the large increases were going to the local school district. Through blogging about this concept and explaining (over and over again) about the state's complicated school funding formula, I was able to take some of the mystery out of this issue. Readers could then use the blog site's search feature to call up any articles or postings I had ever done related to property tax issues. This provided a sense of history and an archived review for newer readers.

DISADVANTAGES TO BLOGGING

I've spent some time extolling the virtues of being a school leader who blogs. But what about the disadvantages? I must acknowledge some drawbacks to blogging.

Written words can be misunderstood. Much successful communication is based on nonverbal communication. People's gestures and facial expressions provide valuable context and background for the spoken word. In an online environment, the absence of these nonverbal cues can cause problems.

Complicating the issue further is the anonymous nature of many online interactions. In face-to-face interactions, we often know some of the background and perceived motivations of the individuals we're interacting with. In the rough-and-tumble world of online communication, this is seldom the case. Written words are often misinterpreted and seldom softened by the subtleties and niceties of personal contact. These difficulties are then compounded by the complexities of typing and navigating the technological aspects of the online medium. Because keyboarding can be awkward and even tedious for many people, they tend to get straight to the point—and that point is often blunt, and even rude at times. When people don't take the time for the personal kindnesses that can accompany personal interactions, the cold hard facts and opinions dished out in online chat rooms and discussion boards can provoke the worst in people. Most people who frequent online boards usually develop thick skin pretty quickly—or they leave and do not come back. As is true of most technological innovations, the social changes usually drag along behind the technology. It will be interesting to see if people become more socially aware and sensitive in online environments or whether we just adapt and accept the perceived bluntness of the online environment.

You can't run from the controversy. When a patron raises a controversial issue to a school leader in private, the ripples are small and often the leader has some time to determine a course of action to respond to the patron's concerns. But in the "instant gratification" world of Internet interactions, any controversial issue is aired in front of hundreds or even thousands of readers, often before the moderator or administrator of the blog has even seen the question or comment. Then the leader's response to that question or issue is immediately apparent to all who lurk in the background as readers. The speed of these interactions is far greater and they are farther reaching than such traditional forums as letters to the editor of the local paper. Sometimes the speed of these interactions can play to the leader's advantage, but in many cases it can be problematic.

It takes time. Blogging takes time. There's no way around it. This may be the most frequent question I get from school leaders who are thinking about blogging—the busy school leader wonders where to find time to blog during his or her frenetically paced work life.

While blogging does take time, this is not as big a problem as most people think. Under normal circumstances, a blogging superintendent or principal can plan on spending anywhere from 10 minutes to an hour a day blogging. The time spent can vary widely based on the leader's comfort level with blogging technology and the type of blogging he or she chooses to do. Most of the blogging software—Blogger, Typepad, LiveJournal, and others—has become so user-friendly that new bloggers can be up and blogging live in 10 minutes or so.

What inevitably happens, though, is that the blogger gets interested in the more advanced features that are now available and spends extra time playing with audio blogging and video clips, and making the site more attractive by adding third-party features such as stat counters, weather stickers, and other miscellaneous extras. But this is really part of the fun of blogging, and most bloggers do not consider this as part of the time commitment for actual blogging content. In districts where the leaders have access to technology experts, such added matters are farmed out and the leader can concentrate almost exclusively on the content for the site.

While blogging does take time, this is not as big a problem as most people think. . . . Most blogging leaders develop some type of routine so that blogging becomes integrated into daily work life.

Most blogging leaders develop some type of routine so that blogging becomes integrated into daily work life. Here is a typical day when I was a blogging school superintendent.

Day in the Life of a Blogging Superintendent

This is a composite view of numerous experiences I've had with blogging. All of these are real, though they're combined from several different experiences.

7:23 AM— ◆ I tossed my coat on the table, turned on the computer, and sat down at my desk with a steaming cup of black coffee. I took a careful sip and, while the computer loaded, checked my inbox for any notes or handouts from Jim Evans, our director of finance; Joy Goshert, our curriculum director; or Wendy Hite, our director of special education. These talented individuals, who were part of our management team, often placed articles or Web links in my basket as potential fodder for the blog.

Sure enough, on top of the stack was a copy of an article Jim had printed about an alternative view of America's alleged obesity crisis. The article took potshots at legislation that was trying to require schools to record the body mass index (BMI) of every student and then report these data to the state department of education. Indiana legislators were currently considering just such a bill. Reading the article, I noted several good points and several assumptions that seemed wrong-headed to me. I noted the URL, then turned to the computer and found the online version of a related article. I then started a blog post describing a position on the issue and hyperlinked to the online legislation so that patrons could see the actual bill that required schools to track and report students' BMI. I reminded them that they could use the Legislative Sticker on the sidebar of the Web site to contact their legislator by e-mail if they had an opinion about this bill.

7:35 AM— ◆ I finished the blog post, ran the spell checker, and read it one more time. Satisfied, I clicked "post" and sent the message off into cyberspace. I then clicked "view blog" so I could see what the patrons would see when they accessed the blog site. I grimaced when I noticed an awkward sentence, immediately went into edit mode, corrected the sentence, and then republished the post. I went back to the "view blog" button, clicked it, and read the new version. Much better. I let it stand.

7:42 AM— ◆ I slurped the now lukewarm coffee, turned to the stack of mail in my inbox, and waded into it.

8:25 AM— ◆ Looking up from my mail, I glanced out the window and wondered if there had been any reaction to my postings. I refreshed the screen on the blog site and saw two patron comments. Scrolling down the post, I noticed the first commenter took a slap at the lunches in his child's school; the second comment noted that the legislation should be enacted. Noticing that neither poster had asked any direct questions or indicated they needed a response from me, I decided not to respond.

1:35 PM— ◆ After a round of meetings and conferences, I returned to the office and briefly checked the site again between phone calls. Nothing new, though the stat counter showed that there were several thousand more hits on the site.

2:00 PM— ◆ I spent the remainder of the day returning phone calls, answering e-mails, and talking to several principals.

8:37 PM— ◆ While surfing the Internet at home, I checked the blog site one more time. Seeing nothing unusual, I checked the weather report for the next day and headed for the easy chair and the evening newspaper to unwind.

This account pretty well sums up a normal day of a blogging superintendent. While it's difficult for any school administrator to describe a "typical" day, this is a fair representation of how much time blogging takes when things are somewhat normal. I believe that the time I've spent blogging was in most cases a wise investment.

In addition to the ever-present concern over time, another potential disadvantage for the blogging school leader is the use of the technology itself.

TROUBLE FOR THE TECHNOPHOBE

Despite the user-friendly style of most popular blogging software, the truly technophobic leader may still find this whole business of blogging a little awkward at first. I've found that most of the free blog sites have gone to point-and-click versions that generally require nothing more than making menu selections to get started. In the early days of blogging, a person needed some knowledge of HTML language (the code used to build Web sites) to make changes to the sites. However, current software requires very little background in technology other than a basic familiarity with computers and a little awareness of how online interaction works.

Since many teachers and students are now blogging, it is not unusual for blogging school leaders to turn to others for some support when they get stuck. For most new bloggers, though, the tough part isn't getting started, but a bit later on, when they become sufficiently comfortable to want to start customizing the site to make it more personal. This is when it becomes easy to fritter away 2 hours playing with some third-party function such as adding a new statistics counter to keep tabs on traffic to your site.

DEALING WITH ANONYMITY

For most school administrators, the potential for an anonymous "lurker" to spew negativity on a blog site is perhaps the most fear-provoking aspect of blogging. While superintendents and other school leaders tend to grow somewhat calloused to detractors, the idea of intentionally opening up and allowing such a free environment to exist is counterintuitive for many leaders. School leaders have traditionally played turtle to such negativity, quietly pulling into their shell and hoping the negativity goes away.

We're living in a new age, folks! It's not going away. If you don't have a current established and controlled forum for dealing with such negativity openly, then the negative person can easily open up his or her own site and spew negativity in unrestrained and uninhibited fashion. By having an established blog site with established readers, the blogging leader can set up a positive, interactive stage that will flush out the negative individuals and in most cases expose them to the wider public. The negative poster often believes that many people think like he or she does. When a negative poster puts up a comment that takes a slap at someone or something going on in the school system, in many instances it is immediately pounced on by other individuals with a contrary view. While the blog moderator posts the initial content, it is often the give-and-take of readers' opinions that brings people back to the site again and again.

Leaders who are beginning a Web log should consider starting it with the comment features turned off, especially if the fear of negative comments is a major concern for them. It's much easier to turn the comments on later and open up the forum than to start out by allowing comments and then turn them off when controversy strikes. The politically savvy school leader will recognize that community patrons will view such a move as censorship or, even worse, think their leader is too thin-skinned to handle a little controversy on the discussion board.

GETTING STARTED

So you think you want to be a blogger now? Getting started is quite simple.

Step 1. Inform your superiors. Inform your immediate supervisors—your school board or your superintendent—about your intentions and why you want to blog. Be sure you've read numerous blogs and taken careful note of the style and format of blogging. Make sure you're clear as to whether your superiors understand your purpose for blogging and who you're attempting to represent when you blog. Is this to be a personal blog? Will you be representing yourself, the school, or the school district? The higher your leadership position, the more difficult it is to separate your personal views from the views of your organization. After presenting my initial blog site to the school board in a public board meeting, our board asked me to put a disclaimer on the site indicating that I was representing my own personal views and did not claim to represent the school board or any individual board member's views. This is an

The higher your leadership position, the more difficult it is to separate your personal views from the views of your organization.

excellent idea so that you aren't perceived as putting your superiors out on a limb on a particular topic or view that they might not share with you.

Step 2. Choose your blogging software. There are many different blog sites that offer free or inexpensive blogging software and free hosting for your blog content. Start by checking out Blogger, LiveJournal, TypePad, or others; check out the features and any potential costs.

In most cases, blog sites will allow you to set up a blog and try it out. In addition, you can usually delete the entire blog at any time. You can also set up the blog so that only the people you identify can access it. This is an excellent way to get started if you want to experiment, without your blog being visible to everyone on the Internet.

Step 3. Set up your site. There are many choices to make when setting up your Web log. Most of these choices are menu-driven and do not require any technical background to get started. To help the neophyte, when you come to a setting that you do not understand there are usually default choices that present the most standard and popular settings. The range of decisions goes from the basic colors and font styles of how your blog will look, up to the way your blog will archive all your posts. Almost all the choices you make can be changed later when you get more comfortable with how the blog software works. The average person who is somewhat familiar with computers can be up and blogging in 10 minutes.

Step 4. Decide how much public interaction you want. These are the most important decisions that a school leader will make when deciding to blog. There are many options available when deciding what type of public interaction you will allow on your blog. These options range from no public comments at all and limited public visibility, to unlimited anonymous public comments and unlimited public visibility on the Web, from a very restrictive and limited public presence to a wide-open public forum.

—*No public interaction and limited public visibility on the Web.* The blogger can decide to leave the comment functions turned off and allow only selected individuals the ability to view the blog. This means that not only is the communication on the blog site one-way, but only a few individuals will be given the ability to access the site. The blogger who is just getting started might consider providing access to only a few invited people and even leaving the comments function turned off. This option might be ideal for the new blogger who is not only nervous about the public visibility, but also might be nervous about how blogging works and whether he or she will have the discipline to keep the blog current. There isn't much use for this type of blogging except for the experimental benefits. However, if the blogging experiment fails, only a few people will know you even tried!

—*Limited public interaction with limited public visibility on the Web.* In this scenario, the blogger leaves the public comments open, but only allows selected members to be able to access the blog. An example might be a superintendent who wants to experiment with the blog site but provides access only to administrators while working out the bugs. In this case, the blog site would be password-protected; only individuals who were invited would be able to see the blog site. They would, however, be able to use the comment function to leave comments for the other invited members to see. A typical use for this type of blog might be a family scattered across the world that wants to keep up with each other but doesn't want the rest of the world looking at their pictures and commentary. Many family blogs are set up this way. This option is a viable choice for the blogging leader who is experimenting but doesn't want to make the blog openly visible, yet would like to see how the comment functions work.

—*No public interaction but open public visibility on the Web.* In this scenario, the blogger would choose to leave the public comment function turned off but would leave the blog open to any person in the world who might stumble across the site. This is the most common and perhaps the best way to get started for a school leader who is semi-comfortable with blogging software and the use of the blog site, but wishes to ease into the rough-and-tumble world of Internet interactions. It is easier to turn on the public comment function later on a specific post. The blogging leader who intends to use the blog site as a kind of online newsletter might choose this option.

—*Open public interaction with blog moderator approval and open visibility on the Web.* In this scenario, the blog moderator would allow patrons to leave comments, but only after the comment is e-mailed to the moderator, who must approve the comment before the blog site allows it to be posted. This is a good option for getting started, but it does require the blog moderator to monitor e-mails frequently. As a blogging superintendent, I started out this way but quickly grew tired of approving every comment. After a while, I simply changed the settings for comment approval and allowed all comments to be posted. The blog moderator will still have to monitor the blog closely, because there will be situations where some comments will have to be deleted. In this option, the blog site is openly visible on the Internet, but the comments posted by the public require prior approval.

—*Open public interaction for registered users only and open public visibility.* The next-least restrictive option would be to leave the public comment features turned on but require the commenter to register. In this scenario, the commenter can still be anonymous, but he or she must register and provide an e-mail address. Of course, the commenter can still use an e-mail address that does not identify the individual, but it does discourage the "drive-by" negative commenter because the person has to go to the trouble of registering first. The blog site would still be visible to anyone.

—*Open public interaction and open public visibility.* This is the most common blogging format. In this scenario, the blogger would leave the comments function on and would allow open public access to the site. Any person who stumbled onto this site would not only be able to see the blog site but could also leave an anonymous comment. This type of blog promotes the highest readership and creates the most community input. It also provides an open forum for every person, and hence must be monitored regularly.

OTHER DECISIONS TO MAKE

When you have some blogging experience under your belt, there are other options to consider. You might consider adding a statistics counter to keep track of the number of visitors to your site. If you find that you have enough visitors, you might also consider adding advertisements as a means of generating revenue for your organization. Other options include adding weather stickers, links to other educational organizations, or even polling software. There are many third-party add-ons that can make your blog site more attractive and more interesting to your readers.

EXPANDING YOUR READERSHIP

The greatest and most attractive Web log in the world is useless without readers. Once you've become comfortable with blogging and are ready to expand, it's time to increase the traffic to your site. There are several ways to do this:

E-mail the link to your employees. Start by e-mailing your link to all your employees; ask them to bookmark the site or consider making it their home page on their school computers. The key to expanding your readership starts with getting your employees to check the site regularly. You can also ask them to forward the link to others they know in the community—even to the parents of their students.

Mention the site in multiple public forums. I promoted my blog site by demonstrating it in several public school board meetings so that the local press would pick up on it. The local papers followed by writing articles about the blog. I also mentioned it in various Kiwanis Club and Rotary Club presentations to get the word out among community leaders. You can also advertise the site in the many school newsletters that go home to parents. For at least a year or more, you will want to continually mention the blog site in as many public forums as possible.

Make your site a "one-stop shop." Good blogs are gateways to rich information from a single site. Consider including on your blog links to all your parent grade portals, school Web sites, local newspapers, weather channels, athletic organizations, school calendars, and so forth. The more links you provide, the greater chance that a patron will come to your site first.

RSS Feeds. Putting an RSS feed on your site can help to increase traffic. An *RSS feed* is a simple piece of software that can be used in a news aggregator to notify a reader that you have updated information on your blog site. A *news aggregator* is a software program that collects the news that patrons are interested in. This saves time because people don't have to visit each Web site or blog site in which they're interested. Using this technique, a patron can put your site on his or her news list and be notified by e-mail whenever you post new information.

Why Blog?

Blogging is just one more tool for the communication-oriented school leader. It will not replace conventional public relations strategies, nor is it a good choice when a leader is already under siege. Yet it remains a very powerful tool for interacting with the community in our high-tech age. Our constituents are growing accustomed to communicating in a fast-paced digital world. The more avenues we can provide to educate and inform the public about the important issues that affect our schools and our children, the better chance we have of sustaining and improving our public schools.

Remember, if you don't start blogging *to* them, they may start blogging *about* you!

CHAPTER EIGHT

A WHOLE NEW MIND FOR SCHOOLS

DANIEL H. PINK

There are two kinds of people in the world, an old joke goes: those who believe that everything can be divided into two categories—and the rest of you. Human beings somehow seem naturally inclined to see life in contrasting pairs: East versus West, Mars versus Venus, logic versus emotion, left versus right.

Yet in most realms we usually don't have to pick sides—and it's often dangerous if we do. For instance, logic without emotion is a chilly, Spock-like existence. Emotion without logic is a weepy, hysterical world where the clocks are never right and the buses always run late. In the end, yin always needs yang.

This is especially true when it comes to our brains. The two sides work in concert—two sections of an orchestra that sounds awful if one side packs up its instruments and goes home. As Chris McManus (2002) puts it,

> However tempting it is to talk of right and left hemispheres in isolation, they are actually two half-brains, designed to work

together as a smooth, single, integrated whole in one entire, complete brain. The left hemisphere knows how to handle logic and the right hemisphere knows about the world. Put the two together and one gets a powerful thinking machine. Use either on its own and the result can be bizarre or absurd. (pp. 183–184)

In other words, leading a healthy, happy, successful life depends on both hemispheres of your brain.

But the contrast in how our cerebral hemispheres operate yields a powerful *metaphor* for how individuals and organizations navigate their lives. Some people seem more comfortable with logical, sequential, computer-like reasoning. They tend to become lawyers, accountants, and engineers. Other people are more comfortable with holistic, intuitive, and nonlinear reasoning. They tend to become inventors, entertainers, and counselors. And these individual inclinations go on to shape families, institutions, and societies.

The contrast in how our cerebral hemispheres operate yields a powerful metaphor for how individuals and organizations navigate their lives.

Call the first approach *L-Directed Thinking.* It is a form of thinking and an attitude to life that is characteristic of the left hemisphere of the brain—sequential, literal, functional, textual, and analytic. Ascendant in the Information Age, exemplified by computer programmers, prized by hard-headed organizations, and emphasized in schools, this approach is directed *by* left-brained attributes, *toward* left-brain results.

Call the second approach *R-Directed Thinking.* It is a form of thinking and an attitude to life that is characteristic of the right hemisphere of the brain—simultaneous, metaphorical, aesthetic, contextual, and synthetic. Underemphasized in the Information Age, exemplified by creators and caregivers, shortchanged by organizations, and neglected in schools, this approach is directed *by* right-brained attributes, *toward* right-brained results.

Of course, we need both approaches in order to craft fulfilling lives and build productive, just societies. But the mere fact that I feel obliged to underscore that obvious point is perhaps a further indication of how much we've been in the thrall of reductionist, binary thinking. Despite those who have deified the right brain beyond all scientific evidence, there remains a strong tilt toward the left. Our broader culture tends to prize L-Directed Thinking more highly than its counterpart—taking this left-brain approach more seriously and viewing the alternative as useful but secondary.

This is changing, however—and the change will dramatically reshape our lives. Left brain–style thinking used to be the driver and right brain–style thinking the passenger. Now, R-Directed Thinking is suddenly grabbing the wheel, stepping on the gas, and determining where we're going and how we'll get there. L-Directed aptitudes—the sorts of things measured by the SAT and deployed by CPAs—are still necessary, but they're no longer sufficient. Instead, the R-Directed aptitudes so often disdained and dismissed —artistry, empathy, taking the long view, pursuing the transcendent—will increasingly determine who soars and who stumbles. It's a dizzying—but ultimately inspiring—change.

Unfortunately, this epic shift in the direction of R-Directed Thinking is not to be seen in most of our schools. When museum curators of the future assemble an exhibit on American schooling in the 20th century, they'll have many artifacts to choose from—chunky textbooks, dusty blackboards, one-piece injection-molded desks with wraparound writing surfaces. But one item deserves special consideration. I recommend that in the center of the exhibition, enclosed in a sparkling glass case, the curators display a well-sharpened No. 2 pencil.

If the global supply chain ever confronted a shortage of No. 2 pencils, the American education system might collapse. From the time children are able even to grasp one of these wooden writing sticks, they use them to take an endless battery of tests that purport to measure their current ability and future potential. In elementary school, we assess children's IQs. Later on, we measure their skill in reading and math—then plot their scores against children from the rest of the state, the country, and the world. By the time kids arrive in high school, they're preparing for the SAT, the desert they're told they must cross if they hope to reach the promised land of a good job and a happy life. This SAT-ocracy has its virtues, but America's test-happy system also has several weaknesses that are only recently being acknowledged.

For example, Daniel Goleman, author of the groundbreaking book *Emotional Intelligence* (1995), has examined an array of academic studies that have attempted to measure how much IQ (which, like the SAT, measures pure L-Directed Thinking prowess) accounts for career success. What do you think these studies found? Grab a No. 2 pencil and take a guess.

According to the latest research, IQ accounts for what portion of career success?

a. 50 to 60 percent

b. 35 to 45 percent

c. 23 to 29 percent

d. 15 to 20 percent

The answer is between 4 and 10 percent. (Confining oneself only to the answers presented is a symptom of excessive L-Directed Thinking.) According to Goleman, IQ can influence the profession one enters. My IQ, for instance, is way too low for a career in astrophysics. *Within* a profession, however, mastery of L-Directed Thinking matters relatively little. More important are qualities that are tougher to quantify, the very kinds of high-concept and high-touch abilities I've been mentioning—imagination, joyfulness, and social dexterity. For instance, research by Goleman and the Hay Group (Goleman, 2002) has found that within organizations, the most effective leaders were funny (*funny ha-ha*, that is, not *funny strange*). These leaders had their subordinates laughing three times more often than their managerial counterparts (and humor depends heavily on the brain's right hemisphere). But where have you seen a standardized test that measures comedic aptitude?

Actually, you could find one in New Haven, Connecticut, where a Yale University psychology professor is developing an alternative SAT. Professor Robert Sternberg (2003) calls his test the Rainbow Project—and it certainly sounds like a lot more fun than the pressure-packed exam many of us endured as teenagers. In Sternberg's test, students are given five blank *New Yorker* cartoons and must craft humorous captions for each one. They must also

---

More important are qualities that are tougher to quantify, the very kinds of high-concept and high-touch abilities I've been mentioning—imagination, joyfulness, and social dexterity.

write or narrate a story, using as their guide only a title supplied by the test givers (for example, "The Octopus's Sneakers"). In addition, students are presented with various real-life challenges—arriving at a party where they don't know anybody, or trying to convince friends to help move furniture—and asked how they'd respond. Although still in its experimental stages, the Rainbow Project has been twice as successful as the SAT in predicting how well students will perform in college. What's more, the persistent gap in performance between white students and racial minorities evident on the SAT narrows considerably on this test.

Sternberg's test doesn't aim to replace the SAT, only to augment it. (In fact, one of its funders is the College Board, which sponsors the SAT.) And the SAT itself has been revised to include a writing component. But the Rainbow Project's very existence is revealing. "If you don't do well on [the SAT]," Sternberg (2003) says, "everywhere you turn [the] access routes to success in our society are blocked." As more educators are recognizing, however, those roadblocks can exclude people with aptitudes that the SAT does not measure.

This is especially true for high-touch abilities—that is, the capacity for compassion, care, and uplift—which are becoming a key component of many occupations in our Conceptual Age. The number of jobs in the "caring professions"—counseling, nursing, and hands-on health assistance—is surging. For example, while advanced nations are exporting high-tech computer programming jobs, they are importing nurses from the Philippines and other Asian countries. As a result of this shortage, nursing salaries are climbing and the number of male nurses has doubled since the mid-1980s (Weintraub, 2002).

What does all this mean for you and me? How can we prepare ourselves for the Conceptual Age? On one level, the answer is straightforward. In a world seemingly defined by so many variables beyond our control, in which L-Directed Thinking remains necessary but no longer sufficient, we must become proficient in R-Directed Thinking and master aptitudes that are high concept and high touch. We must perform work that overseas knowledge workers can't do more cheaply; that computers can't do faster; and that satisfies the aesthetic, emotional, and spiritual demands of a prosperous time. But on another level, that answer is inadequate. What exactly are we supposed to do?

Here's a thought: What's the most prevalent, and perhaps most important, prefix of our times? *Multi.* More and more of the jobs in our economy require multitasking. Our communities are multicultural. Our entertainment is multimedia. While detailed knowledge of a single area once guaranteed success, today the top rewards go to those who can operate with equal aplomb in starkly different realms. I call these people "boundary crossers." They develop expertise in multiple spheres, they speak different languages, and they find joy in the rich variety of human experience. They live *multi* lives because that's more interesting and, nowadays, more effective.

Mihaly Csikszentmihalyi (1996) has uncovered a related dimension of the boundary crosser's talent: those who possess it often defy traditional gender-role stereotyping. In his research, he found that "when tests of masculinity/femininity are given to young people, over and over one finds that creative and talented girls are more dominant and tough than other girls, and creative boys are more sensitive and less aggressive than their male peers." This bestows unique advantages, according to Csikszentmihalyi. "A psychologically androgynous person in effect doubles his or her repertoire of responses and can interact with the world in terms of a much richer and varied spectrum of opportunities" (p. 9).

Think about this: In any symphony, the composer and the conductor have a variety of responsibilities. They must make sure that the brass horns work in synch with the woodwinds, that the percussion instruments don't drown out the violas. But perfecting those relationships—important though it is—is not the ultimate goal of their efforts. What conductors and composers desire—what separates the long remembered from the quickly forgotten—is the ability to marshal these relationships into a whole whose magnificence exceeds the sum of its parts.

What has become more valuable is what fast computers and low-paid overseas specialists cannot do nearly as well: integrating and imagining how all the pieces fit together.

So it is with the high-concept aptitude that I refer to as Symphony. The boundary crosser, the inventor, and the metaphor maker all understand the importance of relationships. But the Conceptual Age also demands the ability to grasp the *relationships between relationships*. This meta-ability goes by many names—systems thinking, gestalt thinking, holistic thinking. I prefer to think of it simply as seeing the big picture.

Seeing the big picture is fast becoming a "killer app"—a must-have quality—in the business world. While knowledge workers of the past typically performed piecemeal assignments and spent their days tending their own patch of a larger garden, such work is now moving overseas or being reduced to instructions rendered in powerful software. As a result, what has become more valuable is what fast computers and low-paid overseas specialists cannot do nearly as well: integrating and imagining how all the pieces fit together. This ability has become increasingly evident among entrepreneurs and other successful businesspeople.

For instance, one remarkable study found that self-made millionaires are four times more likely than the rest of the population to be dyslexic (Gill, 2003). Why? Dyslexics struggle with L-Directed Thinking and the linear, sequential, alphabetic reasoning at its core. But just as a blind person may develop a more acute sense of hearing, a dyslexic's difficulties in one area may lead him or her to acquire outsized ability in others.

As Sally Shaywitz (2003), a Yale neuroscientist and specialist in dyslexia, writes, "Dyslexics think differently. They are intuitive and excel at problem-solving, seeing the big picture, and simplifying. . . . They are poor rote reciters, but inspired visionaries." Game-changers such as Charles Schwab, who invented the discount brokerage, and Richard Branson, who has shaken up both the retail music and airline industries, cite their dyslexia as a secret to their success. It forced them to see the big picture. Because of their difficulty analyzing the particulars, they became adept at recognizing the patterns.

Michael Gerber (2003), who has studied entrepreneurs of all sorts, has reached similar conclusions: "All great entrepreneurs are Systems Thinkers. All who wish to become great entrepreneurs need to learn how to become a Systems Thinker . . . to develop their innate passion for seeing things whole."

Both academic studies and firsthand observations are showing that pattern recognition—understanding the relationships between relationships—is equally important for those of us who are not intent on building our own empire. Goleman (1998) writes about a study of executives at 15 large companies: "Just one cognitive ability distinguished star performers from average: pattern recognition, the 'big picture' thinking that allows leaders to pick out the meaningful trends from a welter of information around them and to think strategically far into the future." These star performers, he found, "relied less on deductive, if-then reasoning" and more on the intuitive, contextual reasoning characteristic of Symphony.

This rapidly shifting terrain is already prompting some archetypal L-Directed workers to recast who they are and what they do. As one example, Stefani Quane of Seattle calls herself a "holistic attorney"—dedicated to taking care of your will, trust, and family matters by viewing them in context rather than isolation, and examining how your legal concerns relate to the entirety of your life.

The capacity to see the big picture is perhaps most important as an antidote to the variety of psychic woes brought forth by the remarkable prosperity and plentitude of our times (if, that is, you are among the haves rather than the have-nots). Many of us are crunched for time, deluged by information, and paralyzed by the weight of too many choices. The best prescription for these modern maladies may be to approach one's own life in a contextual, big-picture fashion—to distinguish between what really matters and what merely annoys. As I discuss in the final chapter of *A Whole New Mind* (Pink, 2005), this ability to perceive one's own life in a way that encompasses the full spectrum of human possibility is essential to the search for meaning.

In addition to seeing the big picture, the ability to encapsulate, contextualize, and emotionalize has become vastly more important in our Conceptual Age. When so much routine knowledge work can be reduced to rules and farmed out to fast computers and smart, L-Directed thinkers abroad, the more elusive abilities embodied by what I call Story become more valuable.

In many ways, stories are how we remember. As the cognitive scientist Mark Turner (1996) writes in *The Literary Mind,*

> Narrative imagining—story—is the fundamental instrument of thought. Rational capacities depend on it. It is our chief means of looking into the future, of predicting, of planning, and of explaining. . . . Most of our experience, our knowledge, and our thinking is organized as stories.

As important as stories have been throughout history, however, they have taken a backseat to facts in recent times. Stories amuse, but facts illuminate and inform. Stories divert, but facts reveal—and on and on. The problem with that view of things is that it runs counter to the way our minds actually work. And today, minimizing the importance of stories places you in professional and personal peril.

Findings facts wasn't always as easy as it has become today. A great deal of the vast store of the world's information was piled on the dusty shelves of physical libraries. Today, though, facts are ubiquitous, mostly

When facts become so widely available, each one becomes less valuable. What begins to matter more is the ability to place these facts in context and to deliver them with emotional impact.

free, and available at the speed of light. What's unsurprising today would have seemed preposterous just 15 years ago. These revolutionary developments are glorious—but they have enormous consequences for how we work and live. When facts become so widely available, each one becomes less valuable. What begins to matter more is the ability to place these facts in *context* and to deliver them with *emotional impact.*

That is the essence of the aptitude of what I call Story with a capital S—context enriched by emotion. Story exists where high concept and high touch intersect. Story is high concept because it sharpens our understanding of one thing by showing it in the context of something else. To paraphrase E. M. Forster's famous observation, a fact is "The queen died and the king died." (When you think about it, memorizing just those kinds of facts was commonplace for most of us when we took history classes in school.) But a story is "The queen died, and the king died of a broken heart." Story calls on a different part of us and, in so doing, plants such stories deep within us. As Terry Deal (2008) wrote in Volume 4 of this series,

> Google is a splendid resource for getting information—but it is not a replacement for a good story. We remember stories. Embedded in the narrative are important lessons and triggers for our emotions.

Likewise, as more people lead lives of greater abundance, we'll have a correspondingly greater opportunity to pursue lives of meaning. And stories—the ones we tell *about* ourselves, the ones we tell *to* ourselves—are often the vehicles we use in that pursuit.

A nascent movement known as "organizational storytelling" aims to make organizations aware of the stories that exist within their walls—and then to use those stories in pursuit of organizational goals. Take Steve Denning, for example. Denning began his career as a lawyer and later become a mid-level executive at the World Bank. "I was a left-brain person," he says. "Big organizations love that kind of person."

But Denning was booted from his job and banished to the organizational equivalent of Siberia: a department known as "knowledge management," corporate jargon for how a company organizes its vast reserves of information and experience. As he sought to understand what the World Bank knew—that is, what knowledge required management—Denning discovered that he learned more from trading stories in the cafeteria than he did from reading the bank's official documents and reports. An organization's knowledge, he realized, is contained in its stories. And that meant that if he was really going to be the top knowledge honcho at the bank, he had to go well beyond the L-Directed lawyer-executive approach he'd learned in the first 25 years of his career. So he made the World Bank a leader in knowledge management by making it a pioneer in using stories to contain and convey knowledge.

"Storytelling doesn't replace analytical thinking," Denning (2001) says. "It supplements it by enabling us to imagines new perspectives and new worlds. . . . Abstract analysis is easier to understand when seen through the lens of a well-chosen story." Now Denning is spreading his message—and telling his story—to organizations worldwide.

Here's another example of the potency of Story in people's everyday lives: Today, at Columbia University Medical School, all second-year medical students take a seminar in narrative medicine in addition to their hard-core science classes. There they learn to listen more empathically to the stories their patients tell and to "read" those stories with greater acuity. Instead of asking a list of computer-like diagnostic questions, these young doctors broaden their inquiry. "Tell me where it hurts" becomes "Tell me about your life."

The goal of this radical new approach is empathy, which studies have shown declines in students with every year they spend in medical school. And the result is both high touch and high concept. Studying narrative—listening to Story—helps a young doctor relate better to patients and to assess a patient's current condition in the context of that person's full life story. Being a good doctor, Charon (2001) says, requires narrative competence—"the competence that human beings use to absorb, interpret, and respond to stories."

The board that accredits medical schools now makes communicating effectively and empathically with patients a factor in a student doctor's overall evaluation. That may seem like a commonsense move—and it is—but in the heavily L-Directed medical profession, it's a sea change. In the meantime, stage actress Megan Cole travels to medical schools across the United States teaching a course called "The Craft of Empathy."

Let me suggest here that educators at all levels—teachers and building-level principals and superintendents and professors—can put the power of Story, and of listening to stories of children and parents and patrons of schools, to good use each and every day.

We *are* our stories. We compress years of experience, thought, and emotion into a few compact narratives that we convey to others and tell to ourselves. That has always been true. But personal narrative has become more prevalent—and perhaps more urgent—in a time when many of us feel called to seek a deeper understanding of ourselves and our purpose.

More than a means to sell a house or even to deepen a doctor's compassion, Story represents a pathway to understanding that does not run through the left side of the brain. We can see this yearning for self-knowledge through stories in many places—in the astonishingly popular "scrapbooking" movement, where people assemble the artifacts of their lives into a narrative that tells the world, and maybe themselves, who they are and what they're about, and in the surging popularity of genealogy as millions search the Web to piece together their family histories.

What these efforts and many others reveal is a hunger for what stories can provide—context enriched by emotion, a deeper understanding of how we fit in and why that matters, and the enormous healing power of *empathy*. The Conceptual Age can remind us, if we will listen, of what has always been true but rarely acted upon—that we must listen to each other's stories and that we are each the authors of our own lives, as well as a powerful force in the lives of every person we meet.

Source: From *A Whole New Mind* by Daniel Pink, copyright © 2005 by Daniel H. Pink. Used by permission of Riverhead Books, an imprint of Penguin Group (USA) Inc.

REFERENCES AND RELATED READING

Charon, R. (2001, October 17). Narrative medicine: A model for empathy, reflection, profession, and trust. *Journal of the American Medical Association.*

Csikszentmihalyi, M. (1996). *Creativity: Flow and the psychology of discovery and invention.* New York: HarperCollins.

Deal, T. (2008). Leadership on a teeter-totter: Balancing rationality and spirituality. In P. D. Houston, A. M. Blankstein, & R. W. Cole (Eds.), *Spirituality in educational leadership* (Vol. 4 of *The soul of educational leadership* series). Thousand Oaks, CA: Corwin.

Denning, S. (2001). *The springboard: How storytelling ignites action in knowledge-era organizations.* Boston: Butterworth-Heinemann.

Duthie, A. D. (2003, March 3). Future SACT may test creativity. *Badger Herald* via University Wire.

Gerber, M. (2003, August 17). The entrepreneur as a systems thinker: A revolution in the making. *Entreworld.*

Gill, C. (2003, October 7). Dyslexics bank of disability. *Courier Mail* (Queensland, Australia).

Goleman, D. (1995). *Emotional Intelligence.* New York: Bantam.

Goleman, D. (1998). *Working with emotional intelligence.* New York: Bantam.

Goleman, D. (2002, March 27). *Remarks at the annual meeting of the Human Resource Planning Society,* Miami Beach, FL.

McManus, C. (2002). *Right hand left hand: The origins of asymmetry in brains, bodies, atoms, and cultures.* Cambridge, MA: Harvard University Press.

Pink, D. (2005). *A whole new mind.* New York: Riverhead Books.

Shaywitz, S. (2003). *Overcoming dyslexia.* New York: Knopf.

Sternberg, R. J. (2003, April). The other three R's: Part two, reasoning. *American Psychological Association Monitor.*

Turner, M. (1996). *The literary mind: The origins of thought and language.* London: Oxford University Press.

Weintraub, A. (2002, June 3). Nursing: On the critical list. *Business Week.*

Winters, R. (2003, October 27). Testing that *je ne sais quoi. Time.*

ENDNOTE

EDWARD B. FISKE

Quite a few years ago, when I was covering education for the *New York Times,* I set out to write a story on the remedial writing program at the Borough of Manhattan Community College. I received permission to sit in on an early morning class with a talented teacher who had been assigned a section of the basic writing course containing about a dozen of the school's most academically challenged students.

Having welcomed the students and encouraged them to sit in a circle, the instructor began telling about what he had done that morning—how he had awakened, shaved, had breakfast, traveled to the college, and so forth. I began wondering what all of this had to do with the teaching of writing. After several minutes of this personal autobiography, the instructor asked the class, "Would anyone else like to tell us about what they have done today?" After a bit of silence, a young lady slowly raised her hand and avowed that, yes, she would be willing to do so. She then proceeded to tell about a tense ride she had had on the subway into Manhattan. She had boarded the train near the end of the line and was alone in the car until a man entered. She described for the class the thoughts that went through her head and the emotions she felt as she wondered whether she was in physical danger and, if he were to approach her, what she would do. Fortunately, she recounted, the man proved to be no threat, other passengers entered the car, and the trip went smoothly. When the young lady finished her story, the instructor looked her in the eye and said something to the effect of "Do you know what you just did?" She shook her head, looking puzzled. Then he answered his own question: "For the last few minutes, you have been using the English language to keep all of us in this class-room on the edge of our seats." The young lady looked stunned, then pleased.

When the class was over and the students had departed, I sat down with the teacher to discuss what I had just observed. This was a writing class, I pointed out, but at no point did anyone put pencil to paper or chalk to blackboard. And what, I asked, was the point of the telling of personal stories? He replied that an essential prerequisite to writing—any kind of writing—is that the author must believe that he or she has something to say. These students, he continued, had been so beaten down by the environment where they were raised and by the schools they had attended that, in their heart of hearts, they did not really believe they had anything worth communicating. Before he could teach them about grammar and style and voice, he had to go back to the *real* basics. He had to convince them that they had something to say.

The eight chapters in this volume represent a treasure trove of wisdom on how educational leaders can become effective communicators and use such skills to advance the cause of public education. The various authors have described important techniques, from the strategic use of e-mail to the importance of having a single authoritative voice in crisis situations. They have laid out the key principles that inform effective communication. From their various vantage points, they have stressed the importance of transparency, honesty, and integrity. They have repeatedly argued the importance of listening skills. They have reminded us again and again how important it is, in Paul Houston's words, to "tell stories and craft metaphors." I'm glad that I resisted Bob Cole's invitation to contribute one more chapter to this volume, for, quite frankly, I have nothing to add to what these eight authors have already said.

We need educational leaders who can ground both their policies and their public writing and speaking in a broad vision of the new challenges that face public education in the early 21st century.

I would, however, like to build on the experience I just described at the Borough of Manhattan Community College to offer a few thoughts on the matter of content. This is not to suggest that, like the students whose class I observed, education practitioners and policy makers are diffident about whether they have something to say. Far from it. The techniques and principles described in the preceding chapters are essential to communicating important information and ideas on issues ranging from curricular goals to enrollment policies. But there is another dimension of effective communication that we also need from our educational leaders. We need educational leaders who can ground both their policies and their public writing and speaking in a broad vision of the new challenges that face public education in the early 21st century.

When asked by young people about the best way to prepare for a career in journalism, I invariably respond with praise for the liberal arts. For journalists, a liberal arts degree—the particular major does not really matter—might be thought of as a trade school course of study. Consider the skills that a working journalist needs. She must start with an innate sense of curiosity and a propensity to ask a lot of questions. She needs a set of research and other skills to track down the answers to these questions, and she needs to develop the verbal and writing skills to communicate these answers to others. And, perhaps most important, she needs the ability to put whatever story she is working on within a *context*. Depending on the nature of the particular story, this context may be historical, sociological, psychological, economic, or otherwise. These are the perspectives and skills that are fostered by a liberal arts education: breadth of knowledge combined with the ability to look deeply into whatever challenge comes along and, of course, to communicate these insights in an effective manner.

While the skills and values of a liberal arts education have always been the most practical training for a journalist, they are becoming increasingly relevant across a wide range of professions. Just about any professional person these days—from academics to health care workers to politicians to businesspeople—must learn to deal with rapid change and new global perspectives. All of this is a roundabout way of saying that while it is incumbent on educational leaders today to possess solid communication skills, we also expect them to be able to ground what they have to say in a profound sense of context. The context within which teachers, principals, superintendents, and educational policy makers operate is changing in significant ways that students, parents, policy makers, and the general public need to understand.

The nature of the changing context of education today is too complicated to discuss in a short essay, but let me cite three obvious examples. For one thing, we are asking schools to accomplish a task for which there is no precedent. Throughout much of the

20th century, the task of schools was to equip the vast majority of students with the knowledge and skills that would keep them employable for a working lifetime. True, we needed some students with higher-order thinking skills—"metacognition," in current parlance—but we didn't really need all that many of them. In today's rapidly changing world, however, these have become *entry-level* skills. Schools are being asked to educate *every* child to a level that in the past was required of only a few.

Another key characteristic of the new context is that it is global. The ease with which people, products, services, money, and ideas now move around the world is reshaping virtually every aspect of our individual and competitive lives, including the nature of education and the needs of the workforce. Today's young people need all of the traditional knowledge and skills, such as numeracy and literacy, but they must also develop new abilities, such as the capacity to work in teams, to speak other languages, and to understand and be comfortable with other cultures.

Third, there is the issue of access. The United States dominated the world economy for most of the 20th century, in large measure because we educated more of our young people to higher levels than any other developed country. By the 1980s, however, other countries began to surpass us in both the proportions of students completing high school and in the proportions going on to higher education. There is no way that the United States will continue to prosper if, as we are currently doing, we fail to educate nearly a third of our young people.

I like the notion with which this volume opened, namely that, unlike their counterparts in the business world, school leaders lack the power to control their raw materials. I tend to think of their power as comparable to that of governors and college presidents—the power not to control but to set agendas and to persuade.

Principals, superintendents, and other leaders of our schools and districts are in a position where they are privy to policy discussions but also have the ears of students, parents, and local policy makers. They need powerful communication skills to carry out their jobs, and they will be most successful when they use the power of their words and images in the service of a vision of where our country's education system has been, where it is now, and where it is going.

INDEX

**CORWIN
PRESS**

The Corwin logo—a raven striding across an open book—represents the union of courage and learning. Corwin is committed to improving education for all learners by publishing books and other professional development resources for those serving the field of PreK–12 education. By providing practical, hands-on materials, Corwin continues to carry out the promise of its motto: **"Helping Educators Do Their Work Better."**

The HOPE Foundation logo stands for Harnessing Optimism and Potential Through Education. TheHOPE Foundation helps to develop and support educational leaders over time at district- and state-widelevels to create school cultures that sustain all students'achievement,especially low-performing students.

 **American Association of School Administrators**

The American Association of School Administrators, founded in 1865, is the professional organization for over 13,000 educational leaders across America. AASA's mission is to support and develop effective school system leaders who are dedicated to the highest qualitypublic education for all children.